Great Money Saving Tips

Practical Ideas From
Professional Money Managers

by
Jay and Julie Hawk

First edition.

Published by Jellyhawk Financial Press

Copyright © 2018 Jay and Julie Hawk

www.thefxperts.com

All rights reserved. This book or any portion thereof may not be reproduced or used in any manner whatsoever without the express written permission of the authors except for the use of brief quotations in a book review.

ISBN-13: 978-1987747676
ISBN-10: 1987747676

DEDICATION

This book is dedicated to our dear family who loved us, believed in us and encouraged us to excel in our chosen professions

JAY AND JULIE HAWK

TABLE OF CONTENTS

	Dedication	iii
	Table of Contents	v
	Acknowledgements	viii
	Foreword	ix

PART I: FINANCIAL BASICS

1	Introduction to Saving Money	Pg #1
2	How Saving and Investing Money Differ	Pg #7
3	Becoming Wealthy The Easy Way	Pg #9
4	Developing a Financial Plan	Pg #13
5	Opening a Savings Account	Pg #25

PART II: MONEY SAVING TIPS

6	Personal Money Saving Tips	Pg #35
7	Family-Oriented Saving Tips	Pg #75
8	Home Financing and Saving Tips	Pg #99
9	Personal Loan and Credit Card Tips	Pg #111
10	Retirement Savings Tips	Pg #123
11	Parting Advice	Pg #127
	About the Authors	Pg #129
	Index	Pg #131

JAY AND JULIE HAWK

ACKNOWLEDGMENTS

This book is the product of many years of personal experience and research obtained by working as finance professionals, advisors and money managers, as well as from handling our own personal finances. We want to thank those who brought us up, those who gave us the opportunity to learn about finance, and those who encouraged us to start writing based on our experience.

JAY AND JULIE HAWK

FOREWORD

Their extensive professional experience in the financial, banking, mortgage, business, real estate and legal fields — as well as their personal involvement in managing their own money and that of others — have given the authors of this book a sound basis and excellent qualifications for offering you top level financial wisdom on the important subject of saving money.

"Great Money Saving Tips: Practical Ideas From Professional Money Managers" now comes to you from two world-class financial experts with over 40 years combined experience working in the financial industry and then another 20 years writing about various aspects of it for a public audience.

This creatively-illustrated volume marks their sixth book on financial topics published by Jellyhawk Financial Press, with their other titles primarily focused on the financial markets, including guides on how to trade the stock, forex commodity markets. They have also published a two volume series on fundamental and technical analysis for financial markets traders.

Using their extensive financial background and deep experience working with a variety of investment techniques, the authors have now put together a compendium of their best personal financial wisdom as it relates to saving money. The numerous tips in this book can be used by a wide spectrum of people working in different fields, countries and walks of life who share the common goal of saving and stretching their money. This informative book shows the reader many creative and yet completely practical methods of saving money and cutting costs that can be applied in their daily lives and/or as part of an overall long-term savings plan.

The savings techniques and other financial suggestions offered in this book have also been personally tested and proven to work by the authors in their own lives. In addition to saving money, Great Money Saving Tips touches upon a variety of other key financial topics that directly relate to your financial well-being and can also end up saving you considerable amounts of money each year, as well as contributing greatly to your financial and personal security. The extensive number of money saving techniques in this book also cover just about every important angle on saving money, with a special focus on those that directly relate to the personal accumulation of wealth and spending reduction.

Great Money Saving Tips was inspired by the authors' direct experience managing their own and other people's funds as they made and managed investments in real estate, stocks, bonds, deposits, Treasuries and other financial instruments, as well as running and investing in several businesses. They now provide this exceptionally useful information on personal finance to the general public since they feel it could really help others regardless of their financial situation, just as it has helped them find financial independence in their own lives.

Furthermore, no matter whether you already have a savings and investment plan or are new to the idea, this book will cover the essentials of strategic financial planning to make sure you get that key information firmly under your belt. It then offers an abundance of money-saving and cost-cutting tips that can be put to use immediately in your lives, and which you can then pass on to your children, family and friends as you develop your own financial wisdom.

The book begins by introducing the concept of saving and describing the differences between investing and saving. It continues with an important chapter on "Becoming Wealthy the Easy Way", and then moves on to how to start developing and implementing a financial plan in the next chapter, which outlines the crucial topics of strategic financial planning and the prioritization of spending activities. The next topic covered in Part I involves how to open the appropriate type of savings account for your needs, followed by a section on how to improve the return on your savings to conclude that part of this book.

Part II of this book then offers the reader an extensive and lively section on personal savings tips, which include many great cost cutting ideas and a long list of very practical money saving techniques that could save you a small fortune on things like: auto repairs, energy costs, clothing, cell phones and food, among other very common spending items. The next chapter focuses on family-oriented savings tips, such as how to save on child care, family vacations and holiday spending, which are all covered in different sections. That chapter also includes how to save money on funerals respectfully, as well as some sound tips for investing inherited money.

The next chapter delves into some broader financial topics many people find exceptionally important. Covered topics include: how to save money in financing a home, as well as how to get a mortgage, save up for a down payment, refinance your home and pay it off with savings. The next chapter then examines using credit cards and managing credit card debt, before covering personal loans and how to avoid the pitfalls of private lending. The next chapter consists largely of important information virtually anyone needs to know about saving money for retirement, while the last chapter in Part II provides some parting advice and summarizes the key ideas that you will want to take away from this book.

The information in the book has been implemented through all economic cycles and gives practical financial tips that can be invaluable to anyone who has the desire and discipline to become prudent with managing and saving their money. Nevertheless, applying cost-cutting techniques only to then spend the resulting savings without making sure to leave some money set aside for a rainy day presents a common issue for some especially impulsive people. This obstacle to effective saving may need to be overcome through psychological training, a strong resolution to reduce impulse spending, and perhaps the use of a personal spending coach.

Remember, effective saving requires both a certain amount of discipline directed toward putting money away, while also paying attention to and wisely moderating your spending habits. Basically, building up your savings will typically require you to retain money from your income each month in a savings account, while also allocating other earned funds in a timely manner toward covering necessary expenses. Only then would it seem wise to allow yourself to spend some of the excess money on non-essentials.

If you can master that process, then the great news is that bolstering your savings in a disciplined way manner eventually opens the door to investing in a house, for example, among other things. A wise home investment can then become a long-term store of wealth for you — as well as a generous inheritance for your children — and which you can also take shelter in, whereas paying rent for housing costs you money but does not offer you the other benefits.

Anyway, we hope that you find the information in this book useful and that reading it helps you save plenty of money as you learn to apply its various financial principles and wisdom in your life. As you proceed, do keep firmly in mind that saving money remains one of the many skills you will need to master on your journey to achieving personal financial freedom. We intend for this book to send you well on your way toward attaining that worthy goal.

In concluding, we want to thank our readers for investing their time and money in this book and to wish them all great success in developing their own savings plans and in meeting their personal financial goals. We hope they enjoy attaining them as much as we have ours.

Jay and Julie Hawk
www.thefxperts.com
Northern California, April, 2018

Part I:

FINANCIAL BASICS

CHAPTER 1: INTRODUCTION TO SAVING MONEY

Saving money remains a subject that far too many people rarely even give a second thought to — except in an emergency perhaps —and typically this works to their disadvantage. Despite the overwhelming majority of people who know they should be putting money away in a savings account, most of them have little or no real saved money to protect their personal situation in case of a financial problem arising. Instead, they might just live paycheck to paycheck without the financial buffer they really should have that savings provide.

This book intends to address that important issue and provide the reader with great, practical tips for saving money in general, as well as providing advice on cutting costs on a wide range of products and services you might wish to pay for during your life. The book will also touch upon key financial aspects you probably need to know related to home purchases, retirement, credit cards, and private loans.

After applying the principles and practices outlined in this book, you should be able to save hundreds — if not thousands — of dollars, pounds, euros and/or yen each and every year of your life, depending on how much and how well you choose to implement these practical ideas.

You will also find the small price you paid for this book and the valuable time you invested in reading it returned many fold as your savings account and spendable income grow as long as you maintain the resolve and discipline to set money aside in a savings plan and cut costs on a regular basis.

Saving in the United States

As an example of the savings deficit that many people face, the grim reality of saving in the United States was covered in a 2017 report by the Federal Reserve entitled, "Report on the Economic Well-Being of U.S. Households."

In the report, U.S. Federal Reserve Board Governor Lael Brainard was quoted as saying: *"The survey findings remind us that many American households are struggling financially, including fully 40 percent of those with a high school diploma or less".*

The Governor continued with, *"More broadly, 44 percent of all respondents could not cover an unexpected $400 emergency expense or would rely on borrowing or selling something to do so. The survey also shows that many adults have no savings for retirement."*

Saving a substantial amount of money is more a matter of how you prioritize your spending, how strong your resolve to save is, and how well you avoid overspending on items you need and want.

The Importance of Saving

The harsh modern reality remains that without developing prudent money saving and cost-cutting habits, you will probably have a hard time saving money, regardless of the amount of income that you are making. This is because many people fall into the financial trap of escalating their lifestyles and spending habits as their income rises without paying due attention to expanding their savings.

Furthermore, due to the material focus of society in many Western countries, like the United States for example, most people are programmed to expand their material possessions over their lifetime. Instead of focusing on getting what they really need, and saving the rest of their income for a more worthy goal, they instead fritter away their time and money on satisfying mere whims, desires and impulses, which ultimately tends to have little net satisfaction associated with it.

Such people have probably also become conditioned to respond to media advertising. This means they tend to be induced to buy the latest smartphone, the latest automobile — and even generally non-essential items like a flying camera drone — before thinking about bulking up their savings accounts like they really probably should be doing instead.

As a result of such savings-adverse habits and conditioning, they typically spend their hard-earned money pretty much as it comes in, and they often end up going into debt to maintain their lifestyle that has become much costlier than it needs to be.

Unfortunately, when harder times come, they then have little to fall back on in terms of financial security. That can result in them becoming destitute, bankrupt and/or financially unable to handle key costs of modern life like rent and/or mortgage payments, which can even result in homelessness. That is exactly where your savings come in, since they will literally "save" you from such financial disasters.

For these good reasons and many more, you really should resolve to stay ahead of the pack by prudently focusing on what you need — instead of what you want — with your expenditures and thereby managing to steer clear of those other far too common financial pitfalls.

Developing Healthy Money Habits

The first part of the book outlines how to develop a financial plan, which anyone can do for themselves and that marks the first step in developing healthy money habits. Strategic financial planning includes making a budget for your future spending, which has always been a great first step when it comes to getting control over your spending habits.

Of course, beginning a savings plan and cutting costs will also be part of a sound financial plan, and that remains the general focus of this book. That planning chapter then outlines how to set goals within a fixed time frame, how to prioritize setting aside a certain amount of money for saving, and how to maintain the resolve to keep saving money when appropriate.

Getting Your Savings Account Started

Once a basic financial plan has been created that you feel determined to stick with, then the next logical step consists of opening a savings account at a bank. Selecting the right bank means doing your due diligence and finding a secure bank with a good credit rating that also offers a decent return on your savings.

Some banks will offer free checking accounts to attract new clients, but those should generally not be using for savings since they often have no interest paid on them and are too easy to use whenever you feel like it. Other banks may charge a small monthly fee for the privilege of maintaining a savings account for you, at least until you have a sufficient balance to warrant them waiving fees and perhaps paying interest on your balance.

Developing Frugality and Cutting Costs

One of the most effective ways to successfully save money is to become frugal and learn some helpful ways to cut costs on the items that you want or need. Frugality means to not spend money unnecessarily or on things that are not needed.

Furthermore, if you resolve to focus largely on satisfying your needs instead of your wants, then most people find that what they need will be taken care of by their other activities in life. This sort of attitude and focus will also allow you to save more money, work less, and become less burdened by possessions as you get older.

The second part of the book will show you many practical ways of being more frugal in your personal and family-oriented financial decisions. These tips typically involve redirecting your spending impulses and desires into less costly ways of satisfying them and remain crucial to saving money over the long term.

Saving Money can Create a Home and Even Save a Life

The later chapters of this book will focus on important savings-related issues like saving for a down payment on a house and getting a home mortgage. Other important topics like taking out personal loans and lending money, managing credit cards and debt responsibly, and saving money for retirement will also get covered.

Basically, after reading this book and resolving to put its sound advice into practice in your life, you can reasonably expect to have more money set aside for emergencies and for key projects you wish to finance.

Another important issue surrounding the practice of saving money involves the fact that having a nest egg or savings account set aside for a rainy day, health issue or a financial crisis like unexpected unemployment becomes far more than just a cliché when you really need it.

Furthermore, unless you have a health safety net of some type or a Good Samaritan just happens to show up on cue, anyone who has had to face a sudden emergency or health crisis without any cash on hand can probably attest to the fact that having funds set aside in a savings account can be a life saver.

Building Financial Confidence

Knowing that you have some extra money saved up can really build your financial confidence when it comes to other undertakings in life. This growing confidence in your financial position also helps build up your prosperity consciousness and attitude toward life that remains truly priceless when you put things into their proper perspective.

As an example of this, if your savings have grown considerably, you can then start to use them for investment purposes to earn even more money in the future. This lets your money start working for you instead of you just having to work for your money, which often becomes the tell-tale sign that your positive wealth creation process has started in earnest.

Basically, by applying the sound financial and money saving principles outlined in this book, you can begin your journey towards financial independence. You will also jump start the process of having sufficient money to fulfill both your and your family's most treasured dreams.

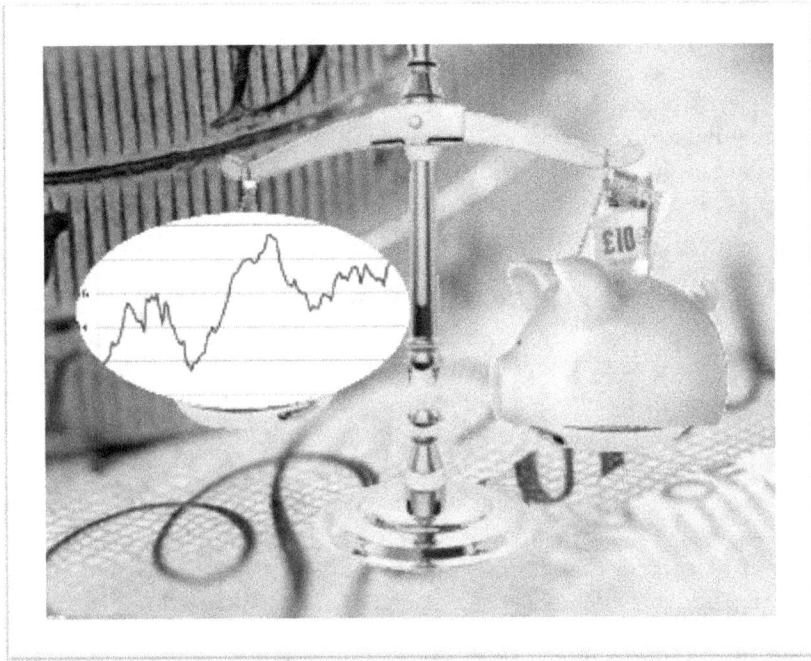

CHAPTER 2: HOW SAVING AND INVESTING MONEY DIFFER

People new to financial matters sometimes appear confused over the differences between saving money and investing money. This seems especially true of those who are relatively new to the typically desirable experience of having more money available to them than they actually require for the necessities of life.

Although these important financial processes are related and should both complement your overall financial portfolio, saving and investing are usually quite distinct from each other.

Furthermore, these two processes for managing your excess money involve different financial skills and levels of expertise when making decisions relevant to each. They also have considerably different objectives and risk profiles. The following sections will clarify how saving and investing money tend to differ.

How Saving Money Works

When it comes to saving money, this process typically involves placing your earned funds into a bank account or into a very low risk, secure and highly liquid into a financial instrument like a certificate of deposit. Such savings accounts and instruments tend to have relatively low returns usually expressed as an annual percentage rate of interest or APR, but then the security and liquidity they offer is usually the desired characteristic.

Unless you are fortunate enough to inherit money, win the lottery or receive a substantial year-end bonus, you might save money over time by making deductions directly from your paycheck. Savings objectives differ, but common savings goals might include putting money aside for a rainy day, a new car, or a down payment on a new home.

Financial advisors often recommend that their clients place into a savings account or certificate of deposit a minimum amount of money to cover six months' worth of basic expenses. This provides a safety buffer for their client, just in case they get made redundant and need money to live on.

How Investing Money Works

On the other hand, investing money typically involves using a portion of your available cash to purchase an asset with the expectation of ultimately making a profit. Investing also usually involves taking a significant amount of risk that the investment might actually lose money in exchange for the chance to earn the anticipated reward.

For example, you might invest your money in a company's stock, a government bond, precious metals, a real estate purchase, expensive jewelry or a collectible item. The prices of these items can rise or fall over time, resulting in a gain or loss relative to your initial investment.

Furthermore, such investments are generally not nearly as liquid as putting money into a savings account, and some investments can even take years to sell or turn a profit. Real estate and collectibles are often especially long term investments, and they also usually involve incurring substantial transaction costs and/or dealing spreads.

Accordingly, you will not want to rely on your investments to provide you with quick cash in an emergency. Instead, your savings will generally be your first line of defense in a financial crisis.

CHAPTER 3: BECOMING WEALTHY THE EASY WAY

Many people born to less fortunate circumstances have bought into the idea that they will never become wealthy unless they win the lottery, are given an unexpected inheritance or receive some other windfall gain. Nevertheless, the truth is that considerable wealth can be achieved relative to your starting point in a much easier and reliable way.

For most people, this relatively easy way to wealth consists of avoiding spending money on unnecessary things and making simple investments so that your money can start to work for you. Some basic tips for becoming wealthy the easy way are covered in greater detail in the following sections.

Let Your Money Work for You

The first thing to remember about becoming wealthy the easy way is that you need to structure your personal finances and assets so that your money is working for you, rather than you working for your money.

If you do choose to be regularly employed by working at a job, at least initially, then make sure you are putting together a savings plan, rather than just expanding your spending to fit your income.

Eventually, your savings plan will allow you to amass enough money for you to retire early as a considerably wealthier person, while your money keeps on working for you.

Small Money Adds Up Over Time

Every penny you save becomes another penny that can work toward your goal of becoming a wealthier person. Of course, that is before the effects of compounding start to boost your growing nest egg even further.

If you do not wish to work harder, then you can begin the process of becoming wealthier by cutting back on all unnecessary expenses — even if you are only saving a small amount. Basically, all of the savings you achieve mean that you will have to work less in future and can retire earlier with the nest egg you have prudently put aside.

Over time, saving only a few pounds a day can add up substantially. For example, saving just three pounds each day for a year adds up to an amazing £1,095, while saving thirty pounds each day will make you £10,950 richer each year.

Avoiding buying that expensive cup of coffee or that pack of cigarettes each day can easily improve your finances considerably over time. Another way to save considerable amounts of cash is to purchase your necessary consumer items, clothes and appliances second hand, while buying groceries in bulk.

Saving Money Buys You Freedom

Once you have accumulated enough money in your nest egg by steadily earning money and at the same time saving a good amount of the money you earn, you may well start to experience the feeling of financial freedom that the wealthy typically enjoy.

At this point, you should only be considering investments that will allow your money to work for you. This means avoiding buying new consumer items, like fancy new cars and clothes that will only rapidly depreciate in value over time. Instead, only invest your money where it will grow over time.

Once your nest egg is earning a sufficient return to pay for the necessities of your chosen lifestyle, then you can consider cutting back on your working hours, perhaps even to the point of retiring entirely.

Taking that step will finally allow you the free time to pursue your life's dreams as a truly wealthy person, so the more money you save, the sooner you can buy your financial freedom.

JAY AND JULIE HAWK

CHAPTER 4: DEVELOPING A FINANCIAL PLAN

Developing a comprehensive strategy for meeting your financial goals is the objective of most personal financial planning exercises. Some people even obtain the advice of a professional financial planner to assist them in this process.

Such planners will typically look over their clients' financial history and their current assets, as well as interviewing the client about what they want to plan for in the future.

This review process allows the qualified financial planner to come up with a list of realistic measures that the client can take to achieve their financial objectives. When adopted by the client, this list becomes their long term financial plan.

The Financial Profiling Process

Financial planners often use questionnaires, conduct in person interviews and review financial documents in order to create a comprehensive financial profile for each client.

This profile typically includes the client's financial goals, their present income streams, current and anticipated expenses, what investments they currently have, their tax history, insurance policies, pension or estate plans, and any other elements relevant to their client's financial status and future.

Additional Consulting Often Helps Complete a Financial Plan

To assist clients with more complex financial situations, the planner may even consult with other professional advisors employed by their client, such as accountants, tax specialists, trustees, bankers and attorneys.

Doing so allows the planner to better understand their client's needs and financial position within its current and historical context. It also helps them propose a strategic financial plan that will not conflict with the client's other investments and/or legal agreements.

When Financial Planning Makes Sense

Most people realize the need for strategic financial planning in their lives when they wish to attain some typically long term goal that requires substantial funding beyond their everyday capabilities.

For example, such goals might include: getting free of debt, purchasing a home or car, retiring, paying for a child's future educational fees, or re-investing funds derived from the sale of major assets like real estate.

Strategic financial planning can also be important and advisable when faced with an unexpected financial windfall, such as an inheritance, large year-end bonus or substantial lottery winnings.

Working With Financial Planners

If you decide to employ the services of a professional financial planner to help you develop a long term financial strategy, make sure the person or company you select is well qualified to assist you properly.

Since they will become familiar with some very personal information you may provide to them, your financial planner needs to come across as trustworthy, professional, well-informed, organized and dedicated to furthering your best financial interests.

Ideally, a good financial planner will also have well-developed presentation skills, since presenting a comprehensive financial plan to a client in a way that engages their trust and cooperation will make the planner far more effective in helping the client achieve their financial goals.

Priorities for Saving Money

Those with a moderate income typically have some funds left over each month to boost their savings after paying for their basic necessities. Nevertheless, they often do not have enough of a financial cushion already set aside to cover major expenses like their children's educational costs or a new car, for example.

If that situation applies to you, learning how best to prioritize your savings activities so that you put money away for the most important purposes first makes excellent sense.

The following sections cover some of the best money saving priorities often suggested by financial advisors for those on a moderate income.

Set Aside Funds for an Emergency

As a top priority for savers or those who are just setting out on their money saving path, make sure you have an adequate emergency fund to cover those unanticipated expenses that may put a significant amount of stress on your finances if they occur.

A rainy day fund can really help you get through tough financial times that can be caused by situations like a protracted illness, involuntary unemployment or car problems, without having to resort to seeking bankruptcy protection or borrowing additional money.

An emergency fund adequate for most purposes should be capitalized with between three and six months of the basic amount that you need to spend each month in order to just get by. The funds should be kept liquid by depositing them safely in a bank account.

Pay Down Debt

A sense of financial freedom is very challenging to achieve without first freeing yourself from debt. This seems especially true of the high interest rate debt that credit card companies often charge on unpaid balances.

Once your emergency fund feels adequate, start saving additional money each month by paying down your outstanding debt burden. If you cannot pay high interest debt off immediately, then commit to whittling it down each month by a meaningful amount.

Avoid living beyond your means during this debt pay-down period, since overspending on luxuries or items you really do not need and cannot afford can easily thwart your best laid saving plans quickly.

Save for Education and Retirement

After you have set aside funds for an emergency and paid down your debt, the next money saving priority for most people will involve depositing money regularly into savings accounts specially created to fund their anticipated educational or retirement needs.

Since educational needs typically arise before retirement needs, they should probably be your next priority if you have children that will need money for college or if you expect to return to school yourself at some point in the future.

Once you have fully funded an account with the money that you expect will be required for future educational purposes, then you can start saving money for when you retire. The amount you need to save for retirement will typically make up the difference between the amount you expect to receive each month from pension plans and your anticipated monthly expenses.

Furthermore, depending on where you live, retirement savings can often be set aside in a tax-deferred account up to a certain limit, so do some research to determine the most efficient way to save for retirement in your particular situation.

Set Money Saving Goals

Now that you are earnestly starting to make a financial plan, prudent money savers would be wise to resolve to take stock of their finances, aim to rein in spending and minimize taxes, and set other realistic financial goals for the next twelve months and the coming years.

The following sections contain some useful tips that you can use to set realistic goals for saving money in future so that you can start the process of making your dreams come true.

Take Stock of Your Finances and Assets

An important step in getting control over your financial situation and setting goals involves taking an accurate inventory of your finances and assets. When it comes to financial assets, this means knowing the cash balances in all of your bank accounts, certificates of deposit and the securities held in your brokerage accounts.

Most people would also benefit from taking stock of their existing assets. If an asset is unnecessary, and you do not want it or anticipate using it again in the near future, you can arrange to sell it via an agent, an auction, a flea market sale, or using online services like e-Bay. This will give you more space and money to help bring the things you do want into your life.

A spreadsheet program like Excel can also be used to help you to organize and compute totals for each type of financial asset you own, as well as the estimated value for the physical assets you own.

Reorganize and Clear Your Debt

An important part of attaining money saving goals will involve avoiding paying high interest rates on debt you might have incurred in the past. If you can pay off any existing high interest rate debt, such as credit card balances, then that would typically make good sense and will save you money in the long run.

You might also be able to consolidate several smaller debts into one larger personal debt at a lower interest rate. Some banks might offer personal or business loans that could be helpful to you in this regard, but be wary of exchanging unsecured credit card debts for debt secured on your residence — even if the rate is lower — since you could end up losing your home if you cannot make mortgage or home equity loan payments in time to stop foreclosure.

Analyze Spending, Set a Budget and Minimize Taxes

Another useful practice for money savers is to look closely at their spending patterns to see if significant amounts of money can be saved over time by changing their expenditure decisions.

Most people trying to save money also find it useful to set a budget for their spending. This allows them to voluntarily rein their spending in once they get beyond the limits they have set for themselves each month.

You can also consult with a tax accountant to see how you might be doing things differently from a financial perspective to save money on the amount of taxes you need to pay.

Set Realistic Goals for Your Saving Plan

It really helps many money savers to keep a desirable goal in mind to promote good savings habits. For example, the start of New Year or a birthday can be an excellent time to set such saving goals for the coming twelve months — and beyond.

Just take some time to review your aspirations for the future so that you can determine what amount of money you will need to save over the coming year to turn those goals into reality.

Furthermore, one of your New Year's resolutions can even be to go through this goal-setting motivational process both for yourself and also for any loved ones that depend on you financially.

Make Money-Saving Resolutions

Making new money-saving resolutions, whether for New Year's, Lent or some other milestone in your life, is an important part of transitioning to a new and better way of saving and behaving with respect to your money. In going through this process, many people will be making resolutions for things that they want to do differently over the coming year and beyond.

If saving money is one of your long term goals, then coming up with some effective money saving resolutions could make sound financial sense for you as part of your overall future prosperity plan.

The following sections offer some helpful suggestions for saving money that might help you make your next year a better and more successful year for your savings related efforts than the previous one was.

Resolve to Increase Your Saving Rate

Increasing your savings rate is one very practical way to enhance your future prosperity. Basically, the more money you put aside each month into your savings account, the faster your nest egg will grow.

One easy way to increase your saving rate involves making a resolution to boost the amount of regular deductions made directly into your savings account from the bank account where you initially deposit your paychecks.

Furthermore, not only can you resolve to be more disciplined about saving money in future, but you can also resolve to avoid tapping into your savings accounts for non-essential purposes. Sticking to both of these money saving resolutions should help boost your savings rate substantially.

Resolve to Save Money When Spending Money

If you are earning a substantial amount of money each month, you probably also spend more than you need to on various luxuries like eating out, entertainment, and non-essential consumer goods or services.

You can resolve to save money when spending money by using discount coupons when dining away from home, going out for recreational purposes, or even just when shopping for groceries. Also consider doing things yourself by developing DIY skills, rather than hiring someone else to do them for you.

Another helpful suggestion for a money saving resolution involves vowing to cut back on any impulse purchases of items that are not necessary for your survival. If you still really want that sort of item, perhaps you can save money by purchasing a similar item from a second hand store instead.

Resolve to Cut Existing Expenses and Debt

Remember, money saved is money earned. Accordingly, if you do not want to spend more of your valuable time working to earn more money, then it makes sense to resolve to take some time to look over your existing expenses closely to identify spending items that you may be able to cut back on or even eliminate.

This process might involve keeping track of your monthly expenses and spending choices either in a more traditional accounting book or in an electronic spreadsheet using computer software like Microsoft's Excel, for example.

Also, the sooner you become debt free, the sooner your savings will start to increase, so learn to live strictly within your means. Resolving to pay off any high interest rate credit card debt quickly, perhaps through a lower rate debt consolidation plan that does not involve trading unsecured debt for secured debt may also make sense for you.

CHAPTER 5: OPENING A SAVINGS ACCOUNT

Once the basic necessities of life have been taken care of, many people decide to open a savings account with their local bank or credit union to help them put money aside for emergency purposes, for their children's education, and to make larger luxury purchases with.

Some savings accounts can be opened with as little as a few pounds, but some banks require a more substantial deposit, so you will need to check with your chosen bank to determine their minimum required initial deposit and make sure you have that amount available when you go to open the account.

A significant advantage of savings accounts over checking accounts is that they typically offer a rate of return on money deposited, which is commonly called the savings account's interest rate. This interest rate usually varies according to changes in some benchmark interest rate, such as LIBOR — the London Inter-Bank Offered Rate.

Simple Steps for Opening a Savings Account

Once you have decided to open a savings account, and have the funds available to do so, the next steps will involve doing some preliminary research and then taking appropriate action to open the account.

Since many banks offer similar savings account programs, perhaps the most important consideration for most people when opening a savings account is the convenience involved in making necessary deposits and withdrawals. Seeing whether banks offer ATM, phone and online access to savings accounts held with them may also factor into your decision.

Another important consideration when contemplating opening a savings account is the interest rate paid and any sign up bonuses offered. For example, some banks will offer a cash bonus for a new account, to eliminate account fees, a relatively high interest rate on balances or a promotional gift in order to attract new savers to deposit money with them.

A good place to start is by doing some research about the terms and incentives for opening savings accounts with your local high street banks that would be convenient for you to use. Choose the savings account option that makes the most sense for your situation.

When you have found the best deal, ask to speak with a new accounts representative at that bank. They will usually ask you to fill out an application form with your contact details and to provide acceptable forms of identification.

You will also need to be prepared to fund your new savings account with a check or sufficient cash to meet the bank's minimum initial deposit requirement for the type of savings account you have selected.

Once your account is open and funded, remember to start a new savings account folder in your files at home. You can place all of the supporting documents, tax information, and subsequent bank statements in this folder that pertain to your new savings account as they arrive.

Viewing Your Savings Account Balance and Transactions Online

If you have Internet access, most major banks will now allow you to view the balance and transactions that have occurred in your savings account held with them via their official websites.

Such websites usually have safe security measures installed that require you to enter a login id, a password and sometimes additional personal information in order to obtain access to your savings account online. If you require this feature, make sure your chosen bank offers it.

Improving Returns on Your Savings

Savings rates, also sometimes called rates of return or simply returns, generally depend on factors like:

- The country you live in,
- The financial institution that holds your savings account for you,
- The amount of time you are willing to forgo making withdrawals for,
- The amount of money you have available for deposit, and
- The level of benchmark interest rates set by central banks.

In the United Kingdom, for example, the benchmark Official Bank Rate is set by the Bank of England's Monetary Policy Committee and reviewed each month. In the U.S., the Federal Reserve Bank's Federal Open Market Committee sets the Fed Funds Rate that acts as a similar interest rate benchmark. After the Great Recession of 2008 that had a global economic impact, these official interest rates were set at historically low levels from which they are still recovering.

As a result, savers in Britain and the United States have become increasingly disappointed with the dismally low interest rates paid by their local banks on basic savings accounts. This situation has driven many people to look for higher deposit interest rates or the better investment yields available from bonds and equities in order to improve the return earned on their savings.

The following sections highlight some of the ways that you could improve the savings rate on your nest egg, with a focus on UK savers, although it should be noted that most of them involve taking greater risks with your money. You may also need to accept some form of reduced access to your funds in order to obtain a better return on your savings.

Higher Yielding Cash Deposit Accounts

In the UK, Cash Individual Savings Accounts or ISAs have offered savers a higher yielding option to traditional savings accounts for some time. These UK based savings accounts allow interest to accumulate tax free on the balance, although a size limitation is placed on them.

From time to time, The UK's Chancellor might announce a modest increase in the tax-free limit for Cash ISAs, so it pays to check with your account or authoritative sources what that limit will be so you can be sure to set the maximum aside in any tax year if that suits your savings objectives.

Nevertheless, ISA savings rates can also vary, and the rates were reduced several years ago when the Funding for Lending scheme was introduced. This program permitted UK banks and building societies to borrow money from the Bank of England for as much as four years to offer better lending rates to companies and individuals.

Since that time, lenders have no longer been dependent on attracting funds from savers, so their Cash ISA rates have fallen notably, although ISAs still typically offer better rates of return for smaller savers.

Another advantage of ISAs is that the Financial Services Compensation Scheme (FSCS) currently covers deposits up to £85,000 with each authorized financial institution. That amount is subject to change, so make sure to determine what level it currently lies at before making a savings decision. In the U.S. savings are insured with the Federal Deposit Insurance Corporation or FDIC up to a current limit of $250,000.

Gilts and Corporate Bonds

Another popular long term option for UK savers that offers a relatively secure investment opportunity is to purchase UK government bonds, which are usually called Gilts and are used to finance Britain's debt programs. Although gilts currently seem quite secure, they are not covered by the FSCS. The equivalent investment for U.S. based savers would be U.S. Treasury Bonds.

These government bonds generally pay a fixed rate or coupon twice per year and give you your invested capital back when they mature. Longer term gilts and treasuries currently have a higher yield than shorter term bonds. This is the most common state of what is known as the Yield Curve, which can rise or fall — and even become inverted — depending on market-driven expectations for interest rate increases or decreases.

For those savers willing to research into the companies involved – as well as take the non-zero risk that they may not get their money back — corporate bonds can offer substantially higher rates of return. In general, these bonds do not offer nearly the same level of security for savers as government-issued bonds though.

Bonds will typically also be rated by a major rating agency like Moody's or Standard and Poor's (S&P), with an AAA rating being the best and a B rating being the worst on the Standard and Poor's scale. Table 1 below shows how investment quality varies between the two rating extremes for the S&P scale.

Table 1

Long-Term Issue Credit Ratings*	
Category	Definition
AAA	An obligation rated 'AAA' has the highest rating assigned by S&P Global Ratings. The obligor's capacity to meet its financial commitment on the obligation is extremely strong.
AA	An obligation rated 'AA' differs from the highest-rated obligations only to a small degree. The obligor's capacity to meet its financial commitment on the obligation is very strong.
A	An obligation rated 'A' is somewhat more susceptible to the adverse effects of changes in circumstances and economic conditions than obligations in higher-rated categories. However, the obligor's capacity to meet its financial commitment on the obligation is still strong.
BBB	An obligation rated 'BBB' exhibits adequate protection parameters. However, adverse economic conditions or changing circumstances are more likely to lead to a weakened capacity of the obligor to meet its financial commitment on the obligation.
BB; B; CCC; CC; and C	Obligations rated 'BB', 'B', 'CCC', 'CC', and 'C' are regarded as having significant speculative characteristics. 'BB' indicates the least degree of speculation and 'C' the highest. While such obligations will likely have some quality and protective characteristics, these may be outweighed by large uncertainties or major exposures to adverse conditions.
BB	An obligation rated 'BB' is less vulnerable to nonpayment than other speculative issues. However, it faces major ongoing uncertainties or exposure to adverse business, financial, or economic conditions which could lead to the obligor's inadequate capacity to meet its financial commitment on the obligation.
B	An obligation rated 'B' is more vulnerable to nonpayment than obligations rated 'BB', but the obligor currently has the capacity to meet its financial commitment on the obligation. Adverse business, financial, or economic conditions will likely impair the obligor's capacity or willingness to meet its financial commitment on the obligation.

Equities and Equity Funds

Some stocks pay a dividend that can be a substantial source of income for savers and can help increase the amount of your nest egg over time. A stock can also appreciate in value, which would further enhance your rate of return. Of course, a stock can also lose value, and it can even become worthless if the company issuing the stock goes bankrupt.

As an alternative, equity funds with a well-established track record provide a way for the less savvy investor to place their savings into a portfolio of equities without having to make specific stock trading decisions. These funds are often also called equity mutual funds and they pool many investors' savings into a single fund that is then professionally managed to optimize collective returns.

Although the fund manager earns a fee for their services, the net investment returns attained by these professionals can often be better than if you were to pick your own portfolio of stocks to invest your savings in.

Prepare to Start Saving Money!

By now you should have a financial plan, have thought deeply about your financial goals, have made some sensible financial resolutions, and have opened up a savings account. At that point, you will have just about everything you need to add to a suitable source of income to start saving money wisely for you and/or your family's future needs, projects and dreams.

The next part of this book will focus on sharing some of the authors' great tips for saving money in various meaningful ways. Putting these sensible money-saving methods into practice in your life will result in more money in your savings account for the things you really want to do, support and manifest in your life.

There really is no better time than **NOW** to get started saving money for your future!

Part II:

MONEY SAVING TIPS

JAY AND JULIE HAWK

CHAPTER 6: PERSONAL MONEY SAVING TIPS

An important thing to remember about saving money effectively is that it typically requires a two-pronged approach that first involves implementing prudent cost-cutting measures to bring your lifestyle in line with your earnings and the budget plan you have devised to manage your spending with.

The second key element of an effective money saving plan involves putting money away in a savings account or another secure investment vehicle for the specific purpose or purposes motivating you to save money in the first place.

Of course, you can perform either money saving step without the other, which is probably better than doing neither, but putting both into practice at the same time typically provides the best and fastest results from a savings perspective.

This key chapter on saving money will focus on the first approach to saving money by offering a series of very practical ways to cut costs in your personal life. Certainly, not all of these practical cost cutting methods will apply to every person at every time in their lives.

Still, they can be useful to keep in mind just in case your own circumstances change so that they become more relevant or if you wish to give advice to others about saving money.

Basically, since a penny saved really is a penny earned, following these tips as part of your sensible and disciplined cost-cutting efforts will save you plenty of money in the long run to spend more prudently.

Also, if you develop the discipline to set aside this money for a particular future purpose, you can use these extra funds to boost your savings account with over time so that you can achieve your financial goals considerably sooner.

Anyway, without further ado, you will find some great tips for saving money on a personal level in the next sections, with the following section focusing on the important topic of cutting costs in your life that will help you save money.

Great Ways to Save Money by Cutting Costs

Saving money is often not just as easy as opening a savings account at your local high street bank. Instead, you need to have extra cash available each month to fund your savings program.

Basically, unless you have a windfall such as an inheritance or year-end bonus, the extra cash you can use to contribute to your savings account will typically come from the money you make over and above what you spend on the necessities of life and any luxuries you might wish to indulge in.

The following sections cover some of the great cost cutting ways to save money that you can use to boost your savings plan without working more.

Saving Money by Spending Less

A great way to increase the amount of money you have available each month for savings is to save money by cutting back on your luxury spending. Reducing travel and accommodation costs for your vacations, as well as entertaining yourself in cheaper ways can boost your savings rate rather quickly.

Furthermore, after housing, food is one of the major monthly expenses for many people. One great way to save money on your monthly food bill is to prepare your own food at home rather than eating out.

You can also eat more economically to save money, perhaps by choosing to eat a wholesome plant-based diet consisting of fruits, vegetables, legumes, grains and nuts, rather than eating more costly meat or other animal products regularly.

Also, it tends to be less expensive to purchase basic food products rather than buying processed food, so considering doing the necessary processing yourself.

Saving Money on Bills

Another great way to increase the amount of money you have available each month for savings is to save money on your recurring expenses like bills.

For example, you might lower your bills by conserving utility resources like electricity, water or telephone use. Consider implementing money saving options like turning off excess lights, especially when they are not being used.

Also, converting to lower wattage light bulbs can make sense, especially when replacing incandescent light bulbs with much more energy efficient fluorescent bulbs.

You can save money on water bills by reducing the amount you water your garden and lawn, as well as by cutting back on toilet flushes and on the amount of water you use when washing dishes.

Scale Back Your Lifestyle

Some people even embark on a substantial lifestyle shift to save money, such as moving to a smaller house or to one located in a less desirable neighborhood. Housing expenses on your current home such as a mortgage or rent can also sometimes be negotiated lower by speaking to your lender or landlord.

Another substantial lifestyle adjustment might involve buying an older and more gas efficient car. Since new cars typically lose as much as 40 percent of their value in the first two years of operation, you can save substantial amounts of cash by buying a used car and letting someone more well off that you take that hefty depreciation loss instead.

How to Save Money by Avoiding Financial Scams

Sadly, some financial predators prey on the innocence, goodwill and caring attitude of unwary investors. The cautious and prudent person interested in saving money will therefore want to make sure that they do not become a victim of any financial scams. Typically, this means only either using insured savings accounts or investing funds wisely in other secure investment products.

Avoiding financial scams typically involves applying a good dose of common sense and not allowing a desire for greater financial wealth to overcome your responsibility to make rational investment decisions with your hard earned money.

The following subsections cover some of the tried and tested ways you can help insulate your financial portfolio from some of the more prevalent financial scams.

If a Deal Seems Too Good to be True…

Many victims of financial scams failed to use realism and critical thinking when assessing the tempting offers of dramatic wealth creation that financial scammers often dangled before them like a carrot before a hungry horse.

Basically, the old adage tends to hold true in that if a financial deal seems too good to be true, then it probably is.

As a result, you should be very, very wary of any exceptionally tempting financial deal, since such an investment "opportunity" is probably actually being offered to you either by a scammer or by a sincere person who is unwittingly working for a scammer.

Ask for Credentials and Independent Verification

One way to avoid falling into a financial scammer's trap is to request their credentials, such as the license or official registration required to offer the financial products they are promoting. If they lack the right credentials, steer clear of whatever deals they might be offering.

Another related suggestion to avoid financial scams involves asking for independent verification of any spectacular returns alleged by the person or company offering you an investment opportunity.

Also remember that it is generally much easier to use your country's legal system to recover funds invested with a local person or company than with a foreign entity, so avoid making financial investments abroad with any but the most trustworthy institutions.

Avoid Letting Greed Make Decisions for You

The main weakness exploited by most financial scammers is an investor's tendency to be greedy. Greed is typically defined as a desire for more than you actually need.

In the case of financial scams, greed might push you towards wanting to earn more money or a higher return on your investment than you really require.

You therefore really need to keep any greedy tendencies very well managed when making investment decisions. Remember to make such decisions rationally in the light of what returns are readily available elsewhere in safe investments.

Finally, always consider the return of your investment capital to be your top priority, and not the return on your investment capital. Applying this key principle alone can help save you from being just another mark on a financial scammer's list of very unhappy customers.

Avoiding Advertising to Save Money

Have you ever felt motivated to spend money after being exposed to some form of advertising aimed at getting you to purchase a product or service — even if you do not really need it? If so, you are certainly not alone.

In fact, an entire, very well-paid industry has arisen to find new and creative ways to market products to the consuming masses in order to maximize their target market's probability of consuming those products.

Why Advertising Presents a Risk to Savers

Many major companies spend large amounts of money promoting their products by using cunning and highly effective advertising programs. These companies' objective in doing so is not to make you happy or financially secure, but to sell their products in order to maximize their profits.

Those who are serious about saving money for some special purpose, like a new home, car, vacation or educational need, could often really help improve their savings rate substantially simply by avoiding consumer based advertising.

This sort of advertising often motivates people to want things that they really do not need, Furthermore, being exposed to such manipulative mental programming can dramatically increase your impulsive spending rate at the expense of your more prudent money savings plan.

Observe the Advertising Around You

If you wish to reduce or even eliminate your exposure to potentially costly advertising campaigns, you can first start to become aware of where you are being exposed to commercial advertising in your lifestyle.

Take note of where you see or hear commercial ads, such as on the television, on the radio, over the Internet, and in newspapers, as well as in public places like transport stations and bus stops. Do your best to avoid being unnecessarily exposed to such advertising.

You can also develop the mental discipline to turn off the sound on commercial advertisements and/or look away from them to avoid being seduced into spending your precious savings money on the product they are promoting that you probably do not really need.

Suggestions for Reducing Exposure to Advertising

Some commercial television stations include considerable amounts of on-air promotional advertising. You can avoid this by switching to viewing only non-commercial television stations that do not promote corporate products in between their regular features.

Similarly, many commercial radio stations will put ads for products sold by their sponsors between the music they play or the talk shows they host. If you do not want to avoid listening to the radio altogether, you can simply change the channel when an advertising campaign comes on the air.

Consider Non-Commercial Internet Media as an Alternative

If you are willing to do some research and have a high speed Internet connection to your computer, you may also be able to watch your favorite serial TV programs on the Internet without ads.

Some people have even completely switched to Internet based media — like YouTube, Netflix or online digital radio stations — for entertainment that typically comes free of commercial advertising.

Another advantage to this sort of Internet media is that it can usually be selected and viewed at will, rather than when it is programmed by a network television or radio stations that usually require the support of commercial sponsors to operate.

Money Saving Shopping Tips

If you have decided to start saving money for some particular purpose, you might benefit from some useful tips that can help you save money when you are shopping for goods and services.

Most sensible money saving shopping tips involve avoiding unnecessary purchases and stretching the money you do spend. This allows you more freedom to buy what you need for your life without wasting the money that you would prefer to save.

The following subsections contain some useful tips that can help you save money when shopping.

Be a Disciplined Shopper

Perhaps the most important step toward saving money when shopping, involves disciplining yourself to avoid those often far too tempting impulse purchases. You can do this by making a list of what you need before you go shopping, and then trimming off any excess from the list before you even hit the stores.

Another important shopping discipline to learn is sticking to a budget that you set either for one particular item or for a group of items, like the food you might buy at the grocery store. Resolve to do your best to manage your spending in a way that makes sense given your income level and savings objectives.

Do Your Homework Before Purchasing

Resolving to research consumer goods you are contemplating purchasing thoroughly before you buy them can help prevent the disappointment of having bought an unsatisfactory product.

Product details and reviews are often available online these days, and you can also research the approximate price you should expect to shell out for the product so that you do not overpay once you have decided to go ahead with the purchase.

Also, since doing your shopping homework takes some time to perform, the delay may allow your initial acquisition impulse to subside sufficiently for you to forgo the purchase altogether. If the item you are thinking of buying is not going to play an essential role in your life, then perhaps you can save money by doing without it.

Buy Used and Care for What You Do Have

The price of quality second hand goods is typically less than half of what you might expect to pay new for the same items.

Shopping for used products to fit a particular need you have identified can be done online via auction sites such as e-Bay and sale listing websites, especially if you know what you want and are confident in the product you are buying used.

If you want to see something before you buy it used, then you may be able to find what you need at various second hand, thrift and charity stores. Another inexpensive source of second hand items is garage, yard and estate sales, as well as flea markets.

Another important money saving tip is to take care of and repair the valuable items that you do have in order to avoid having to replace them.

Preparing Money-Saving Meals

Those operating on a tight budget or wanting to save money for some special purchase can look to cut excess costs from their food budget by preparing money saving meals.

Fortunately for people who are somewhat challenged in the kitchen, saving money on your food preparation costs can be as simple as eating smaller portions or using cheaper ingredients when you make food.

In addition, many money saving meals are also lower in calories and saturated fats than rich restaurant food, so you might also be able to shave a few inches from your waistline in the process. The next sections go into greater detail about money saving ideas you can follow when preparing meals.

Make Smaller Portions, Eat Less Frequently and Fast Periodically

The more food you eat, the more your meals will probably cost you, so cutting back on the amount of food you consume will very likely save you money. This might mean sharing a portion that you would normally eat yourself, or making smaller portions overall.

Eating less could also help you slim down, which might save you having to work the extra calories off at the gym. You could also skip a meal from time to time, or just have a liquid smoothie or shake instead of a solid meal.

Another money saving suggestion is to fast occasionally. Fasting involves not eating food for an extended period, which can be as short as one day or as long as several weeks. Not only can fasting give your bowels a healthful rest, but this practice can also save you substantial amounts of money on food preparation since you do not need to eat at all when you are fasting.

Use Cheaper Ingredients

Processed foods tend to be quite expensive relative to basic foods. They can also contain salt, sugar, various additives and preservatives that can even compromise your health when consumed in substantial quantities over time.

One excellent way to save money when preparing meals is to avoid using processed foods. You can instead start creating your meals from basic foods obtained from the produce section or bulk bins at your grocery store.

For example, you could start preparing a meal with fruits, vegetables, flour, grains and/or oils, and then combine these ingredients with an inexpensive protein source like nuts, beans, peas, lentils or tofu to create a nutritionally well-balanced dish.

Also avoid overdoing the relatively expensive protein or fat in the dishes you prepare, since most nutritional experts now agree that humans need about 80 percent carbohydrates but only about 10 percent of fat and 10 percent of protein in their diets on a caloric basis.

You can also save considerable amounts on your energy bills over time by preparing food in its raw form, rather than cooking it. Many people have found that a raw food diet can also help revitalize your life and improve your overall health considerably; especially if you leave out relatively expensive dairy and meat products and focus primarily on consuming plant foods instead.

Furthermore, the raw plant-based diet works particularly well for those suffering from health conditions like cancer, diabetes, obesity and heart disease, since eating animal products can often result in such problems.

Meat products also tend to be quite expensive relative to vegetable protein sources, so consider replacing them in your meals with plant foods to save money on grocery store bills, as well as on future health care costs.

Buy and Prepare Food in Bulk

Another way to save money on your meals is to purchase the ingredients for one of your favorite recipes in bulk. Volume food purchases are typically cheaper than buying smaller amounts, and certain discount grocery stores cater to those purchasing larger quantities of food.

You can then save both time and money by preparing several portions of your preferred recipe at the same time. These portions can be placed in containers and stored short term in the refrigerator or longer term in the freezer.

For example, beans and rice are a good vegetable protein combination that is relatively inexpensive to buy, but somewhat time consuming to prepare for each meal. They can be cooked in bulk, and then wrapped in tortillas or stored in containers to be frozen.

For a quick and highly cost effective meal, you can just defrost and warm your rice and beans up in a microwave oven and garnish with greens, salsa and tomatoes.

How to Save Money When Dining Out

Dining out regularly can be quite expensive, especially for those on a tight budget. Nevertheless, even thrifty diners might want to enjoy a meal at a restaurant on special occasions with their family, colleagues, friends or clients.

One easy way to cut your restaurant bills is to eat out for lunch or breakfast, rather than dinner. Most restaurants charge considerably more for the offerings on their dinner menu, so you can easily save money this way.

The following sections contain some additional useful tips that might be helpful if you are looking to save money when dining out.

Avoid Ordering Expensive Drinks

Perhaps the most costly component of a restaurant meal, relative to its eat at home value, are drinks. You can often save a considerable amount of money when dining out by simply ordering water rather than soft drinks, hot beverages or juices, and you will most likely do your health a favor as well.

If you want to have an alcoholic drink, such as wine, liquor or beer, with your meal, you may be able to find a restaurant that will allow you to bring your own. This can save you dozens or even hundreds of pounds if you have especially expensive tastes in wine or champagne.

Make sure to call ahead to verify that an unfamiliar restaurant permits this BYOB practice, and enquire whether the establishment will charge a corking fee to open a bottle of wine for you if you have plans to enjoy one at your special meal.

Use Coupons and Ask About Discounts

Many fancy and family restaurants offer specials of the day, often at reduced prices. Some also give discounts to people celebrating a special event, such as a birthday. Ask your waiter or waitress about any specials that might apply when you sit down or call ahead for details.

Another way to save money when eating out is to clip coupons from local newspapers or magazines. Some restaurants also place coupons online at their websites, or at websites that specialize in dining discounts, which you can just print out and bring with you.

Remember to let the person serving you know that you will be using a coupon before you order to make sure that the offer is still valid and applies to your menu selection.

Share Your Food

Many restaurants serve generous portions of rich food or high calorie drinks that are larger than you require. Not only can this be expensive for those on a tight budget, but it can also easily expand your waistline or even make you feel too sleepy to enjoy yourself or work efficiently after the meal.

Instead of overeating or taking excess food home in a doggy bag, consider sharing a meal, drink, dessert and/or appetizer with someone else who likes the same type of food or beverage you do.

Not only does sharing a meal or drink save money, but it can even be quite a romantic thing to do on a special date if you take turns feeding each other choice mouthfuls of delightful food or sipping a shared drink.

Healthy Tips for Saving Money

Your health is one of your most valuable assets. Suffering from poor health can cost you money and eat into your savings, especially if you need to pay for medical expenses or take time off work to recover from an illness.

Furthermore, spending considerable amounts of money on your recovery in terms of drugs or treatment can substantially decrease your savings and reduce your savings rate, even if you have private medical insurance or take advantage of public medical programs like that offered by the National Health Service or NHS in the UK or Medicare/Medicaid in the United States.

It therefore helps to understand and follow some basic ideas of how to maintain your health in good shape and how to treat common health issues at home, rather than running to the doctor or pharmacy for some expensive medicines that often do not work any better.

Money Saving Preventative Health Measures

The old saying goes that an ounce of prevention is worth a pound of cure. You can often prevent the occurrence of more serious health conditions by taking steps to make your lifestyle as healthy as possible. Reducing potentially harmful stress levels by engaging in relaxing activities like meditation can also provide long term health benefits, as can maintaining a healthy weight level.

Some very inexpensive health sustaining tips include following a healthy eating plan, exercising regularly and simple practices like washing your hands regularly. Supplementing your diet with a good quality multivitamin suitable for your age and gender can also help prevent deficiency issues.

For example, the health of many vegetarians and vegans have benefitted notably from reducing the intake of saturated fats found in meat and other animal products that can cause circulatory problems, with vegans benefitting the most. Also, taking regular, but not excessive, exercise helps maintain the fitness level of your heart and lungs.

Another important preventative health measure is eliminating the ingestion of common poisons, like those found in tobacco, some drugs and alcohol products. These are not only expensive to buy and habituating, but the long term cost to your health of using them can be huge.

You can also switch to organically grown produce to reduce your exposure to pesticides that may be harmful to your health, especially when consumed over many years.

Saving Money by Research

If you do have or develop a serious health condition, then taking the time to become a well-informed patient will often save you considerable amounts of money when it comes to treating and caring for it effectively.

The Internet is an excellent resource for researching your diagnosed health condition, as well as your doctor's proposed solution and any inexpensive home remedies that may apply to its treatment.

Money Saving Home Remedies

For those on a tight budget, many money saving remedies for common health conditions exist that you can easily apply at home, once your condition or disease has been properly diagnosed by consulting with a qualified health practitioner.

These home remedies might consist of the application of specific herbs like Aloe Vera for wounds or Echinacea to boost the immune system, as well as homeopathic remedies and simple household products like baking soda, hydrogen peroxide and borax. Also, colloidal silver serves as an excellent natural non-toxic antibiotic, and dietary adjustments like switching to a raw plant-based diet may also be useful for many health conditions.

Some people who prefer alternative health treatments even use drops of highly concentrated hydrogen peroxide in water as a home remedy to treat cancer, especially if they are newly diagnosed and have a slow growing tumor. For an example of this protocol, they might start a two month treatment program by taking one drop of 30 percent by volume food grade hydrogen peroxide in an eight ounce glass of water, then ramp up to 30 drops by month-end, then decrease down to one drop by the end of the second month.

Suitable home remedies can usually be researched online, or looked up in various reference books dedicated to the subject. Most people would be surprised about how effectively many health issues can be treated with items they already have in their cupboards or are growing in their gardens.

Tips for Saving Money on Clothing Costs

Most people end up spending quite a bit of money out of their annual budget on clothes in order to dress themselves up for work, play or entertainment.

Although you might need to buy a certain type and quality of clothing to look presentable at your job, most people can save a substantial amount of money on their clothing costs by following a few simple money saving tips.

The following sections cover some of the more useful tips for saving money on clothing costs.

Buy Second Hand Clothes

New clothing is remarkably expensive compared to the deeply discounted price of good second hand clothes, especially if you do not buy new clothes when they on sale or marked down.

Many charities, such as Oxfam in the UK and the Salvation Army in the United States, offer a wide array of mildly used clothes at their thrift stores that can easily save you hundreds of pounds on your annual clothing budget. Yard sales and flea markets are another inexpensive source of second hand clothing.

Youngsters also grow out of their clothes and shoes rather quickly, so buying children's apparel from second hand shops or accepting handed down clothes from an older child can really save parents a substantial amount of money over time. The clothing savings can then be put aside to pay for more important expenses later on, like the child's education, for example.

Repair the Nice Clothes You Do Have

If you have some really nice pieces of clothing that have seen better days, you may be able to restore them to service with a simple repair, such as sewing on a new button, stitching up a seam or darning holes in wool socks.

Simple sewing tasks like these are really not that hard to master, and taking some time to learn how to repair your clothes can really save you money in the long run.

Furthermore, even if the damaged clothes will never be suitable for formal wear again, you may be able to repair them sufficiently well for them to still be useful as casual clothes to wear for dirty jobs or just around the house.

Avoid Buying or Keeping Unnecessary Clothing

Purchasing excess clothing is often a costly waste of money, and storing excess clothing takes up valuable closet space in your home. Consider each purchase of new clothes carefully and discipline yourself to avoid buying clothing on impulse.

You can also save money and avoid extra work clothing expenses by taking some time to plan out and purchase a set of carefully chosen clothing items that can mix and match with each other to create five professional looking outfits.

Then, just vary your clothing selections as you dress for work each day to create five different outfits for every day of the work week, laundering them as necessary on the weekend.

If you find that you have accumulated excess clothing that you no longer need or want, then consider selling unnecessary clothes at a garage sale, consignment shop or flea market.

Your old clothes may have value to someone else, and you can use the money you receive to save or buy something new. You may also be able to donate your used clothes to a charity in order to obtain a tax deduction that could save you money at tax time.

Saving Money on Cleaning Products

Store bought cleaning products can be quite expensive to use. They can also leave unwanted chemical residues around your house and on your skin or clothing that can compromise the health of your family and pets.

If you have a lot of cleaning to do around your house, you might be surprised to know how much money you can save over time by using relatively safe cleaning products like vinegar, baking soda, and hydrogen peroxide. Even products like salt, rubbing alcohol and even toothpaste have some low cost cleaning applications.

The following sections offer some helpful tips for saving money by replacing relatively expensive chemical laden cleaning products with safe and readily available alternatives.

Save Money by Cleaning With Baking Soda

Baking soda, also known as sodium bicarbonate, is a very inexpensive household cleaning product that is also used in cooking since it is edible in moderate quantities. Baking soda comes in the form of a powder that is alkaline in nature, so it typically helps remove stains that respond to alkalinity.

Baking soda is also abrasive and so it can be used in cleaning applications that require grit to be effective. Some examples of where baking soda can be effectively used as a cleaning product simply by making a paste with water are tooth cleaning and lifting coffee stains.

You can also use baking soda to remove crayon from painted walls by rubbing gently with some baking soda paste on a clean sponge or cloth. Remember not to rub too hard or the paint may erode.

Baking soda can even be combined with coconut oil, cornstarch and some scented essential oils to create an inexpensive natural deodorant, which can save you money too.

Save Money by Cleaning With White Vinegar

White vinegar is an especially pure form of vinegar, which is a highly acidic and sour tasting liquid food product made from the fermentation of ethanol to yield acetic acid.

You can use white vinegar to remove greasy stains on clothes. Just apply a mixture of one part vinegar and two parts water to the stain and wash normally. White vinegar can also remove the soap scum from your bathroom.

Furthermore, white vinegar can be used to take rust stains off a carpet. Take the vinegar and water mixture and apply it to the stain using a spray bottle. After a few minutes, clean the stain off using a brush or sponge and some warm, soapy water.

If your laminated wood floors, windows or glass table tops require cleaning, white vinegar can be effective and safe to use. Just make a more dilute solution by adding a couple of tablespoons of vinegar to a quart of water. Apply this cleaning solution to floors with wrung out cloths and to windows or other glass items by spraying in on and then wiping off with newspaper.

Save Money by Cleaning With Hydrogen Peroxide

As mentioned before under the health care section of this book, where it has numerous applications, hydrogen peroxide is a strong oxidizing agent that is colorless, viscous liquid. In its more concentrated form, it may be used to bleach hair and clothes. The more diluted three percent solutions of hydrogen peroxide have numerous household uses as a disinfectant and cleaning product.

Hydrogen peroxide is used in a special cleaning application to remove blood stains on cloth items that will not bleach out. After testing the item on an inconspicuous place, pour a three percent solution of hydrogen peroxide on the blood stain. Allow the hydrogen peroxide to soak in, and then wash the item out using cold water.

Save Money by Making Laundry Detergent

You can also save quite a bit of money on your laundry bills by making your own laundry detergent. This typically involves using cheap ingredients like a bar of regular soap, washing or baking soda, and water.

The first step in this process involves shaving the soap into thin strips with a knife. These shavings are put in a pot of boiling water to melt into a foamy liquid.

At the same time, you can prepare the washing soda (sodium carbonate) — if you cannot buy it in your store — by heating baking soda (sodium bicarbonate) at 400 degrees in an oven for an hour until it changes consistency.

Both of the above preparations are subsequently mixed with enough water to make it suitable for use as a detergent. This laundry detergent keeps very well if stored in a sealed plastic container.

Save Money by Washing With Water

One of the ways in which people in many countries have been very actively marketed to involves companies promoting the use of unnecessary personal hygiene products. These items are generally toxic, and since you would not usually wish to eat them, you should ideally also not place them on your porous skin.

The good news is that virtually all such products remain unnecessary for most people. For example, most people can simply can wash their hair with cold water, instead of using shampoo and conditioner in order to clean it. Not only does this help preserve your natural conditioning oils, but it also saves money and decreases your exposure to unnatural hair products.

If your hair gets a bit too well-conditioned, then just increase the temperature of the water, and that should rinse some of the natural conditioning oils off. If your hair gets too dry, you can wet it down with cold water and/or condition it with natural oils like coconut or olive oil.

You can also just use water to wash your body with and thereby avoid the use of soaps entirely. This allows your skin's natural conditioners to do their job of keeping your skin healthy. This also means you do not need moisturizers or creams to do that job for you, so you can save money that way too.

More Ways to Save Money on Cleaning Products

Other common household items like salt, rubbing alcohol, dishwashing soap and toothpaste can be used effectively as cleaning products.

Salt can be used to remove red wine stains by placing it on the stain quickly and allowing it to stay there for two hours before washing the stain in cold water.

Ink and lipstick stains can be lifted off fabrics with rubbing alcohol, and hairspray also works well. Apply, then blot the area with a clean cloth and repeat until the stain is largely gone. Lipstick stains should also be scrubbed with dishwashing soap before washing the item

Body odor can be removed from clothes by first spraying them with a half and half solution of rubbing alcohol and water, and then hanging them out on a line to dry.

Crusty white hard water deposits can be removed from glasses by scrubbing with inexpensive white toothpaste and then rising in water. Toothpaste can also be used to clean coins and other metals, although be careful about removing the surface from plated metal items.

Saving Money on Auto Repairs

Automotive repairs can take a substantial chunk out of your savings, especially if the problem involves replacing a major part like the car's engine or transmission. Furthermore, not only are replacement car parts often quite expensive, but labor costs can go through the roof if the necessary auto repair requires a substantial amount of time for a mechanic to complete.

Unfortunately, you can never completely eliminate the risk of having to pay for an expensive auto repair if you want to own and operate a car, especially when the car is outside of its manufacturer's warranty period. Nevertheless, you can take some constructive steps toward saving money on auto repairs, and the following sections discuss some of these in greater detail.

Prevent Repairs With Good Maintenance and Driving Habits

Perhaps the best way to save money on auto repairs is to prevent them from happening in the first place. For example, you can avoid plenty of expensive car repairs that involve costly bodywork and repainting simply by being a careful and alert driver.

Good driving habits include stopping fully when required, avoiding driving in unsafe weather conditions, checking intersections and entering roundabouts carefully, maintaining a safe following distance when behind other vehicles, and checking your car's blind spot and mirrors thoroughly before changing lanes.

Another way to prevent expensive engine repairs is to change your oil regularly and make sure that your car's fluid receptacles are filled to appropriate levels. Low oil levels can result in serious engine problems, and low water levels in your car's radiator can result in overheating. Low clutch or automatic transmission fluid levels can result in gear shifting problems.

Use Only Trusted Mechanics and Get a Second Opinion

Unless you find yourself in an emergency situation, do your best to have mechanics that you trust to work on your car. Basically, the more trustworthy the mechanic you choose, the lower the risk of you being taken advantage of when your car needs repairs.

Preferably, any car mechanic you hire will be a personal friend or family member, although if you do not know a mechanic personally, you can also ask a friend for a reference to a good mechanic that they trust.

Once you have obtained an initial quote for the repairs your car needs from your most trusted mechanic, then consider taking the vehicle to several other repair shops for their opinion on what is wrong with the car and how much it will take to repair it to the standard you desire.

Do Your Research

After your auto's problem has been reliably diagnosed, take the time to do some research of your own to find out how serious the problem is, how much it should cost and how long it should take to repair, and whether there are any quick fixes that you can do yourself to get the vehicle safely back on the road.

The Internet is an excellent place to start doing your homework, since many automotive repair websites exist to which qualified mechanics post solutions to common problems faced by car owners.

One research technique involves just entering the make, model and year of your car — along with a short description of the diagnosed problem —

into your favorite search engine, and then browsing through the results. You can also sometimes ask online experts for their opinion on your car's problem and how much it should cost to repair.

Saving Money When Using Cell Phones

The days of almost universal mobile telephony have finally arrived thanks to the growing cell phone industry, but many people have found the luxury of owning a cell phone to be an expensive addition to their monthly list of regular expenses.

Although your cell phone company will probably not tell you this, many creative ways to save money on your cell phone bill exist. Becoming aware of them can help make calling on the go far more affordable for those living on a tight budget.

The following sections contain some very useful tips for saving money when using cell phones.

Keep it Brief, Prioritize Calls and Text Instead of Call

Friends and family will often talk for far too long when you answer or make a call on your cell phone. Most cell phone companies allow you to specify certain phone numbers as part of an in-calling group that costs you less to communicate with.

You can also aim to prioritize your cell phone usage in order to save your minutes for more important calls when you are out, and defer most personal calls for when you are at home and have more time to chat at less cost.

For example, you could keep personal cell phone conversations as brief as possible, perhaps by saying that you will call the other party back when you are at home and asking when would be convenient to do so. Being disciplined with this practice will allow you to instead use your precious cell phone minutes for important business conversations, emergencies and travel updates.

You can also save considerable amounts of money on your cell phone bill by texting, rather than calling. Basically, the cost of texting is fairly limited and so it cannot quickly expand your cell phone bill like talking to a chatty friend on your cell phone can.

Avoid Contracts and Go Prepaid Instead

Many cell phone companies try to tempt you into signing up for an extended service plan by offering a 'free' phone. Not only might agreeing to this arrangement prevent you from getting a better cell phone deal elsewhere for years, but you may also end up either paying for minutes you do not use or using your cell phone more than you need to in order to eat up your excess plan minutes.

Avoid having to pay this extra monthly bill and save considerable amounts of money in the long run by purchasing a good quality second hand cell phone. You will now own an asset, rather than having the liability of a monthly bill, generally at a much lower overall price.

You can then usually just activate your cell phone with your preferred carrier and buy prepaid minutes instead of having a monthly plan. This will typically allow you to budget and limit your cell phone usage far more effectively.

Use Internet Telephony Services

Another excellent way to save money on your cell phone bill is to use an Internet based phone service instead whenever possible. If you have access to the Internet at your home or at a location that offers Wi-Fi access you can tap into, many smart cell phones, personal electronic devices and computers can operate cheap Internet telephony software and voice apps like Skype, Telegram, Discord, TextFree, FaceTime, Facebook Messenger and Google Voice.

These services typically allow you to make calls to existing contacts who also use the service and are online free of charge. Skype, Discord, Facebook Messenger and FaceTime even offer free video calls to other online contacts if you both have webcams installed.

Getting your friends and colleagues actively connected on these services can save you a lot of extra expense on your monthly land line and cell phone bills, especially if they live in an area that is a long distance call for you, and you all have access to the Internet.

In addition to saving on your cell phone calls, you can also use these online services to make calls to land and mobile telephone numbers, as well as to send text messages. The fees involved are usually quite modest and considerably less than what you would pay to use your cell phone instead.

Saving Money on Energy Bills

As the winter solstice quickly approaches, the colder season will often see a household's energy bill rise significantly compared with summertime power costs. If you are living on a tight budget, this added expense can really eat into your spending money available for purchasing holiday gifts.

Fortunately, those looking to save money on their winter energy bills can readily take some constructive steps toward reducing their power-related expenses. The following sections cover some of the more effective ways to cut back on your winter energy bills.

Saving Money on Heating Costs

Since most of a winter's energy bill will be consumed by heating-related appliances, such as a furnace or hot water boiler, reducing the need for those items to consume power is an excellent place to start when looking to cut down on your power usage.

You can start saving money by turning down your central heating or radiator setting to a cooler temperature. To tolerate such a cooler environment, you can compensate by wearing an extra wool sweater or a cosy robe around the house. Sheepskin boots or heavy wool socks can help keep your feet warm so you feel less of a need to heat up your house.

Selective space heating can also save you money relative to central heating, especially if you tend to occupy just one room in your house for much of the day or night. You can simply run the space heater in that room, while allowing the rest of the house to stay cool.

If permitted in your area, burning wood and paper products that you collect yourself in a wood burning stove or fireplace installed in your home can save you substantial money on heating costs.

Turn Refrigerators Down or Off

Refrigerators cost a considerable amount of power to run, even when the ambient temperature is kept relatively low, so they can contribute substantially to your power costs. This is especially true of older refrigerators that are typically considerably less energy efficient than the more modern fridges.

In addition, you can often save a substantial amount on your power bill by simply turning off your refrigerator, particularly if it is largely used to cool and store preserved drinks or other non-perishables.

Another creative way to cut back on your refrigeration power costs could involve keeping the fridge outside in your garage where the temperature is even cooler than in your kitchen. Since the external temperature will be chilly, the fridge's compressor will need to run less often to maintain a given cooling temperature, thereby saving you money.

Turn Off Lights, Electronics and Appliances

A classic way to cut back on your energy costs is to turn off the power using devices in your home whenever you are not actually using them. While turning off electronics and appliances is generally helpful in cutting power bills, the shorter winter days make the efficient and cost-effective use of lighting even more important at that time of year.

While such measures may not result in as large a savings as that typically seen from reducing your heating and refrigeration expenses, it can really add up over time and usually takes just seconds to implement.

Furthermore, most people in Europe are now switching from

incandescent bulbs to the newer fluorescent and LED light bulbs to provide even more energy savings in the darker wintertime months. Although some people might still prefer to read by an incandescent bulb, and fluorescents are typically difficult to dim, applications like hall, room, exterior and bathroom lighting will often suit the newer and considerably more energy efficient bulb types very well.

JAY AND JULIE HAWK

CHAPTER 7: FAMILY-ORIENTED SAVING TIPS

While almost all families can save money using the personal tips mentioned in the previous chapter, some cost cutting measures pertain largely to groups of people living together and sharing a common financial situation, of which the most common example is a family.

Those managing the finances of a family generally need to consider expenditures related to having children to care for and potentially send to higher education like vocational school, college or university. They might also need to put aside money for family vacations, reunions, funerals, marriages or other significant life events common to many families.

Other family-oriented considerations related to saving money include planning for receiving money as an inheritance and/or giving away an inheritance to your heirs once you pass on.

This chapter will focus on addressing those family-related savings opportunities by offering a series of very practical ways to cut costs and plan financially for important events. While not all of these methods will apply to every person at any particular time in their lives, most people will probably experience the need for this information at some point during their lifetimes, and those who have the foresight to plan ahead tend to cope better with the financial challenges life has to offer.

Reducing Child Care Costs

Recent figures indicate that UK families are now spending over £80,000 more than they were just ten years ago to raise one of their children from birth to the time they are ready to leave for college. That number typically runs even higher for those families based in the United States.

Many parents are also concerned about the impact that the rising cost of child care might have on their standard of living. Child care costs have grown in excess of sixty percent over the past decade in Western countries, and the trend remains higher for the years to come.

The following section contain some money saving tips that can help cut you down on your child care costs so that you will have more funds left over to enjoy vacations and quality leisure time with your family.

Reducing Child Care Costs

The cost of nurseries, babysitting and collective child care has risen sharply in recent years to the point where the average career mother is now working roughly four months out of twelve just to pay for the cost of caring for a child. This means that child care costs are typically eating up more than a third of an employed mother's income.

Although not possible for every profession, working from home may be an option to help your family avoid the high cost of childcare and allow you to spend more time with your child. Furthermore, if the mother's job will not permit this flexible telecommuting work option, then perhaps the father's will.

Child care is typically most expensive for younger children under the age of two. After they are potty trained, the cost of caring for them goes down considerably, and they will qualify for state-funded nurseries at the age of three years.

When your child eventually reaches school age, you will then just need to pay for an after-school club so that you can pick them up several hours after school lets out. You can also arrange for them to participate in sports activities or have a friend or relative help out by caring for them during the after school hours until you get home from work.

Look into Child Care Assistance Programs

Fortunately, many working parents living in developed countries will qualify for some form of child care assistance while their minor children are still living at home. For example, the UK government has recently announced a new tax measure that will allow parents to deduct several thousand pounds per child for child care costs from their income tax bill each year.

State funded nurseries, subsidized nursery fees, working tax credits and employer child care vouchers are all ways that parents can seek to save money on their child care bills. Remember to apply to the appropriate authority for child care assistance as soon as you can to increase your savings.

Consider Self-Employed Child Minders or Relatives

If your local commercial child care facilities are beyond your budget, you may be able to save money on child care by looking for a self-employed child minder. Be sure to ask for personal references and verify that they have sufficient experience to care appropriately for your child.

In the old days, elderly relatives such as grandparents, great aunts or great uncles would often lend a new parent a hand with child rearing. Going this route can both save you money and provide a relative on a pension with some helpful additional income. The child might also benefit from having a loving elder family member care for and advise them wisely.

Money Saving Ideas for Family Vacations

Spending too much money on a family vacation you cannot afford can be even more stressful for some people than just remaining at work. So, when you finally have the chance to take your family on a vacation you are all looking forward to, but your budget is limited, why not look for ways to trim some of the cost of taking a family vacation?

The money you save on your family vacations by being thrifty can be substantial, and it may even help pay for something important like your children's education or a down payment on a new car, for example. The following sections discuss some useful money saving ideas for family vacations.

Consider a Car Trip Rather Than Flying

Airfare can be remarkably expensive these days, especially for a family of three or more people. While you might be able to get a family discount on your airfare, or shop around for the best air travel deal, most family vacations that involve driving to a tourist destination cost substantially less than vacations where flying is required.

Another advantage of driving to your chosen destination with your family car is that you will then be able to visit sights on the way, as well as enjoying the financial benefit of not having to rent a car and pay for auto insurance when at your chosen destination.

Rent a Home or Cabin Instead of Hotel Accommodation

Staying in hotels can be a really expensive way to take your family on vacation. Also, most hotel rooms lack basic living conveniences like cooking and laundry facilities.

If you rent a home or cabin instead of a hotel room, you might not only save money on your family's accommodation, but you could save money by avoiding eating at restaurants and paying to have your family's clothes cleaned while on vacation.

Look for Bargains and Off-Season Vacation Opportunities

If you avoid traveling during peak vacation seasons, like those around most holidays, then you might be able to get a special deal since demand for accommodation at your chosen destination will tend to be considerably lower.

Travel costs may also be reduced during the off-season, especially when it comes to airfare and car rental expenses. Nevertheless, remember that having to endure substantial inconveniences or delays, like switching planes or making travel stops, may cut into your vacation time and make travel substantially less pleasant.

If you are not offered a deal when you make your booking, be sure to ask if any are available, just in case the hotel representative or travel agent knows about some specials intended for more budget conscious vacationers.

Keep Restaurant and Entertainment Costs Low

Eating at restaurants while on a family vacation can be really expensive. Do your best to prepare your own food, perhaps also going on picnics in local parks instead of eating out.

Also consider bringing some mobile entertainment with you that the whole family can enjoy. For example, if you have a portable DVD, video player or video game system, you could bring along some videos for your family to watch together during the evenings or at other quiet times. Lower tech entertainment might include playing board and card games.

Bringing your own entertainment can help you alleviate boredom and save you money since you can avoid paying for expensive entertainment like movies and shows while on your low budget family vacation.

Saving Money on Holiday Meals

As just about any family knows, holiday meals spent with friends and relatives can take a substantial bite out of your festive budget, so learning how to save money when making them and hosting a seasonal dinner party can leave more funds available for buying gifts and spreading good cheer.

Two of the key ways to save money on holiday meals as a family involve planning ahead and asking for help from the family members and other people who might be attending your festive food event.

The following sections will cover some of these tips and more for saving money on holiday meals while still leaving everyone from your family who attends feeling fully satisfied.

Use Cheaper Foods and Prepare Them at Home

Some foods are clearly less expensive than others, so focus on preparing a comprehensive meal from the less costly foods available at your local grocery store.

For example, regular and sweet potatoes do not cost much to buy or prepare, and they can be a filling side dish to any festive meal. Inexpensive desserts like an apple crumble also make sense on a tight holiday meal budget.

Remember to avoid choosing costly processed or pre-prepared food for your holiday menu, and instead take the time to make your own dishes at home, even if you have to prepare the dishes in advance. This will save you a pretty penny on your holiday meal.

Shop Ahead for Bargains

If you have planned your holiday menu in advance with your family, you can shop around among your local grocery stores for deals on the foods you will require.

You might also consider adjusting your festive menu depending on what holiday foods are available at the best prices. Some places also have discount or bulk grocery stores that have even better deals on foods that you can incorporate into your holiday feast, and this seems especially true if you happen to live in a city.

Engaging in a bit of prudent advance planning also means you will have time to order food in bulk from discounted online suppliers.

Host a Potluck Holiday Meal

If bearing the full cost of a holiday meal with family seems overwhelming on a tight budget, you can simply ask for help from the other people that might be attending. Hosting a potluck version of the traditional holiday meal can really help you make the feast so much more affordable and fun.

In many families and groups of friends that enjoy potluck holiday meals together, the host will typically prepare the main course since it often takes the longest to cook. The guests will then usually offer to bring another portion of the meal, such as vegetables and/or side dishes, soup and/or salad, desserts and drinks, with one of the host(s) coordinating who brings what.

Another option for those families on a budget hosting a holiday meal might involve asking attendees to offer a donation to the hosting family for having their holiday food prepared for them.

Save Leftovers and Avoid Preparing Too Much Food

Holiday meals often result in a considerable amount of leftovers, and some of this good food can go to waste if it is not frozen or preserved promptly.

To save even more money, make sure all edible food left over after a holiday meal gets safely refrigerated and then eat it gradually instead of buying fresh food. Even leftover food scraps from people's plates can sometimes be saved as treats for pets to mix in with their regular food.

Another good idea to follow when looking to save money on holiday meals is to reduce the amount of excess food as much as possible. By having a good sense of how many people are going to attend and an accurate idea of how much food they are likely to consume, you can save money by avoiding the preparation of too much holiday food.

Money Saving Holiday Spending Tips

Cutting down on the cost of holiday meals are not the only place where a family can save over the holidays. If the current year's holiday season has turned out somewhat tighter for you financially than you would like, take heart.

The good news is that you and your family can still enjoy the upcoming holiday season and share what abundance you do have with your dear friends and family without draining your bank account or going into debt.

The following sections cover some useful money saving tips to keep in mind and help you stay within your budget when you are making your holiday spending plans for your family.

Smarter Discount Gift Shopping

One way to save money on just about anything is to shop at discounted saver stores instead of at pricier high street stores and indoor shopping malls where store rental costs tend to be higher. Also, look for discounts on specific items you wish to purchase in local newspaper advertisements and then visit that store to buy them.

A very modern way to save money and shop smarter is to shop online for deals, especially if you can get the item you want to buy shipped to you rapidly and have access to the Internet. Most online merchants also allow the use of credit or debit cards to make your holiday gift purchases easier.

If you are convinced that the best holiday shopping deals will come after the peak pre-Christmas rush, you can always give your loved ones gift certificates or checks. Not only does this sort of gift save on wrapping paper, but it also allows them to later spend your gift at popular stores on exactly what they want after prices have been slashed to help reduce inventories.

Budget Your Gift Spending by Person

Have a good sense of how much money you want to spend on each person in your family on your holiday shopping list. Then, simply discipline yourself to keep to your overall budgeted amount when you are out shopping for gifts for them.

Another important aspect of saving money over the holidays is to keep your gift spending budget within your current means, so that you can avoid running expensive credit card balances. This requires that you first take stock of your available cash and then use the desired portion of that amount as your holiday spending budget, to be split among the special people on your gift list.

Also, many people would prefer to get a larger and more valuable gift that they really want, rather than several smaller and less significant presents. Consider asking your gift list people what they would really like for the holidays, rather than just guessing, and then spend your budgeted amount on that item.

Select Holiday Events and Travel Carefully

If being with your loved ones over the holidays requires making extensive and costly travel plans, you might consider having a smaller and more personal holiday celebration at your own home to save money.

You can still reach out remotely to your dear friends and family — almost as if you were there — by getting all the folks you wish to connect to on the holiday to install a free video call service like Skype, Windows Facebook Messenger, Live Messenger or FaceTime. This will allow you to speak with them visually via the Internet so that you can share your holiday parties virtually, without all of the time, cost and bother of travel.

Also, many people get invited to a slew of holiday parties around this time of year, and not just those that involve families. To save time, money and energy, you can be more selective about the ones you actually go to, especially if gifts, food, money or extensive travel is involved in attending. To show your appreciation for the invitation, you can send a nice Thank You note instead of showing up at the party in person.

How Your Grandparents Saved Money

Young people today can often benefit from the wisdom of family elders like their grandparents regarding how they saved money for the important things they wanted in life, like a home, a family or a means of transportation.

While the products available to purchase and invest in have certainly changed in the modern era, many of the money saving principles used by your grandparents still seem relevant to today's younger generations.

The following sections cover some of these principles, but do not hesitate to ask your grandparents — or someone else's — for more useful money saving tips.

Neither a Borrower Nor a Lender Be

In Shakespeare's Hamlet, the elderly Polonius offered to his son the sage advice to "Neither a borrower, nor a lender be". He also provided the explanation that, "for loan oft loses both itself and friend, and borrowing dulls the edge of husbandry."

This advice definitely made good sense in Shakespeare's era, and the same is also true today, especially for those who would like to start saving money. Basically, lending money can result in its loss, and lending money to friends can harm your friendship if they do not pay you back promptly or at all.

Furthermore, when it comes to borrowing, many would-be savers have gotten themselves so deeply in debt — often due to the far too easy use of credit cards — that they cannot effectively save money and service the debt they owe at the same time. Make sure this does not happen to you.

Basically, young people need to learn to live within their means. This process requires you to first spend some time taking stock of your finances in order to come up with a realistic budget, and then developing the discipline to keep your spending inside your budget.

Waste Not, Want Not

Many people are induced by slick advertising campaigns to purchase something new, when what they already have is more than adequate for their needs.

Avoid wasting items and money by using up and wearing out the items you have already purchased, rather than buying new ones to replace them. You can also purchase good quality second hand items to save even more money.

Remember, try your best to ignore the ads, and instead focus on buying what you actually need, rather than what you want, so that your savings will have a chance to increase.

The Best Things in Life are Free

Young people might think that they need to spend money to do almost anything that seems fun, but that just was not the case for their grandparents. Many relaxing pastimes can be done at home for low cost, such as meditation, reading and conversing. Cooking fancy recipes at home can even save you money relative to the higher cost of eating out.

Furthermore, going out for a walk, hike or bike ride are some very inexpensive ways to get out of the house and actively enjoy your surroundings. You can also join a sports team or league if you want to take some more intense exercise.

In times gone by, many people enjoyed observational hobbies like watching birds, fish or even people, as well as playing card and board games. These days, you can also engage in other inexpensive pastimes like browsing the Internet or watching videos on YouTube rather than going out to the movies.

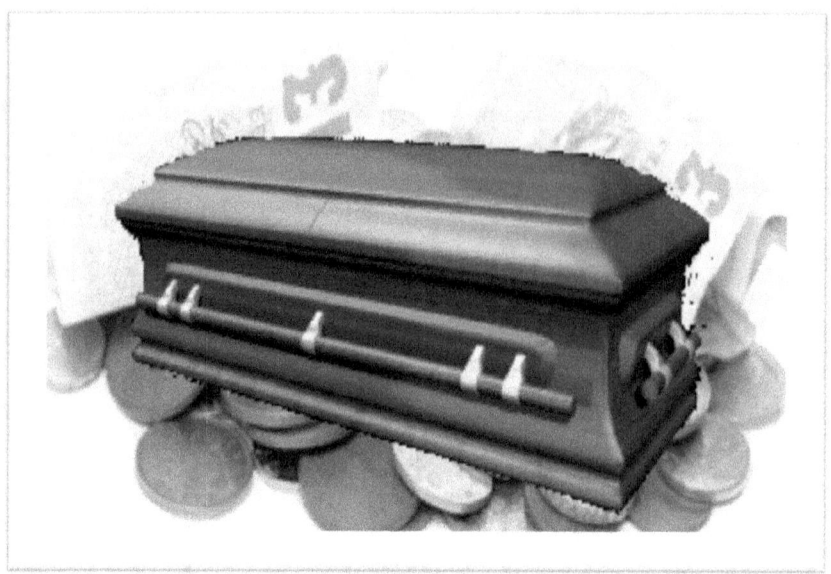

Saving Money on Funerals

Losing a loved one or family member is rarely easy, but it can be even more distressing when you find yourself in a tight financial situation. Unfortunately, preparing for a funeral can be a remarkably expensive affair, especially for the friends and family of the deceased if they plan on holding an elaborate funeral service and wake.

Since bereavement and persuasive funeral home staff can often cloud your judgment when organizing a funeral for a loved one, the best time to think about saving money on funeral costs is before you actually have to. The following sections include some useful tips for saving money on funeral arrangements.

Plan Ahead for a Funeral

One of the most sensible ways to save money on funeral costs is to plan ahead for them. Although accidents certainly do happen, you can resolve to not to leave your bereaved family and friends picking up what can quickly become a very costly tab for your funeral arrangements and your chosen method of being laid to rest.

Planning ahead for your funeral includes making your wishes regarding your funeral known to those who are most likely to be arranging it.

Remember to specify if you would prefer to be cremated or buried, and what time of memorial service and grave marker you wish to have.

Then set money aside to cover these expenses, rather than expecting your loved ones to pay for your funeral. Obtain a realistic cost estimate from a funeral home that you would like to use, and then periodically add to the balance you have saved up to allow for inflation as time goes on.

Shop Around

Before selecting a funeral home, call several conveniently located funeral venues and ask their prices for specific goods and services that the funeral you are planning will require. Depending on where you live, you may be entitled to this pricing information by law.

Once you have narrowed down the funeral home choices over the telephone, you can then visit them in person to obtain an itemized price list, review their facilities and meet with their personnel. It may also save money to have a third party attend such meetings with you who can be more objective about the costs.

Remember, if you are planning for someone else's funeral, do not allow your bereavement and a smooth talking funeral home operator to induce you to spend more than you can afford, purchase unnecessary items, or permit an open ended budget for the funeral expenses.

Choose Economical Funeral Options

Consider shopping for a discounted coffin for your deceased loved one online, rather than buying a coffin from the funeral home at full price. If you do use this method, make sure that the coffin can be delivered in time to be used at the funeral.

Another money saving option involves renting an attractive coffin for the funeral, but burying the remains in a more simple coffin instead. You may even be able to skip the cost of a coffin altogether if the funeral plans allow you to opt for cremation or a cloth burial instead of internment in a coffin.

If cremation is preferred, then ask the funeral home about lower cost alternatives to expensive urns used to store the ashes in. If the ashes are to be scattered, someone close to the deceased may be able to create a container that will give the funeral ceremony a more personal touch.

When it comes to holding a memorial wake, consider making it a less formal pot luck meal hosted at someone's home, rather than a more elaborate cooked or catered affair held at a rented venue. This way, each of those attending the memorial event can help to finance the meal with food that they like to eat.

For additional information about the least costly funeral options, which may save you several thousand pounds on a funeral, you can contact a local memorial society. These organizations are typically listed in telephone directories under funeral services.

Sound Tips for Investing Inherited Money

Once the funeral and grieving has taken place, plenty of people find at least some consolation in the inheritance of money from their departed parents or other loved ones. The giving of a generous post mortem gift in the form of a substantial inheritance can often help assuage the feelings of loss and separation that can arise when a beloved relative or dear friend has passed on.

Nevertheless, the apparently easy money that an inheritance offers can sometimes all too quickly dwindle away into nothing if you do not take some prudent steps to manage your new inheritance with the goal of maximizing its financial potential over the long term.

Those planning to give an inheritance when they pass should also consider carefully whether it would be wise to give it in such a way that their hard-earned money might be wasted instead of put to good use by their heirs.

The following sections offer some helpful tips to follow when investing inherited money that can help you treat your departed loved one's financial gift respectfully and perhaps make it grow even further.

Consider Investment Options Carefully

When you first obtain an inheritance, the temptation can arise to find the first apparently attractive investment opportunity to place it into. This can be particularly problematic if the inheritance was an unexpected windfall.

Unfortunately, rushing into an investment like this at a time when you may be bereaved can have quite negative consequences, especially if you do not properly understand what risks you are taking and what sort of return you can reasonably expect.

If you are unaccustomed to having excess money to invest, you may benefit from the guidance of a professional financial advisor who can help to assess your long term financial goals and suggest how you can best achieve them given your income and newly improved financial status.

Research Any Inheritance Related Tax Issues

Another important issue to consider when inheriting money involves the tax implications of the extra money you are going to be receiving given your particular financial situation.

The tax assessment process is especially important to complete before you rush into any investment opportunity that might tie your inherited money up for a considerable period of time. For example, some people rush to put their new inheritance into paying off their mortgage or buying a new home, when they may end up having to give a good chunk of it back to the taxman.

Basically, taxation is a very personal and unique aspect of inheriting money for you to research carefully with an accounting or tax professional to devise a suitable tax strategy for your particular inheritance. Doing your homework right away will also give you the necessary information you require about what sort of tax liability your inheritance may present, so that you can then invest the balance with greater confidence.

Be Prudent With Your Inheritance

Inheritances can be quickly wasted by burst spending patterns, unwise lending practices and by attempting to take an early, but ill-advised, retirement.

First of all, it may help to remember just how long it took for the person who provided you with the inheritance to accumulate the wealth that they have now given to you. Show appreciation for their savings prowess by not wasting their financial gift on frivolous spending.

Another important aspect of prudent inheriting is to keep your inheritance a secret between yourself, the departed and only those who need to know what you received. Differences in inheritances among family members can sow discord, and crowing loudly about your new inheritance can quickly make you a target for con artists and those offering shady investments.

Finally, avoid quitting your job just because you have now come into some inherited money. Until you have reorganized your finances around getting your new wealth to work for you, you will probably require a regular income to keep paying your bills.

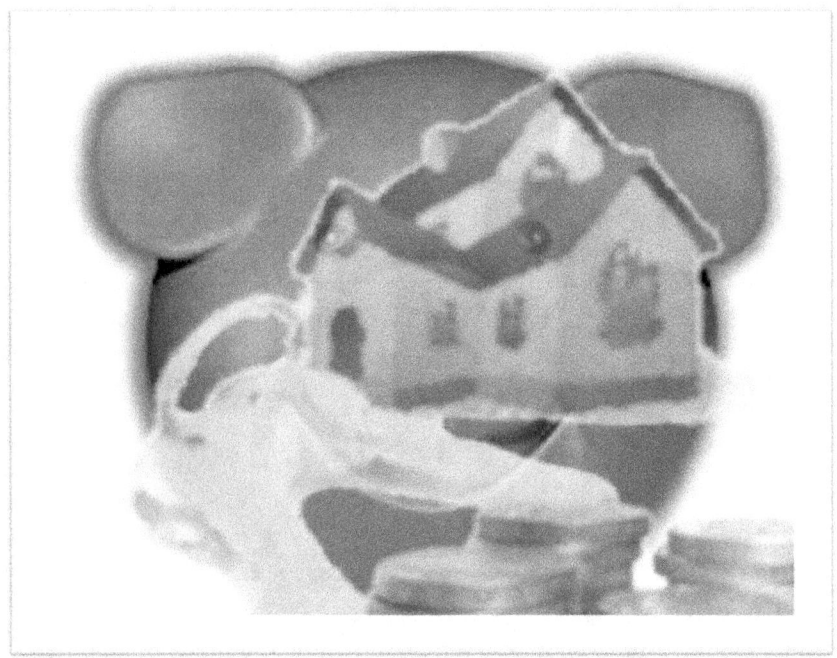

CHAPTER 8: HOME FINANCING AND SAVING TIPS

Although some people are fortunate enough to be able to purchase a home outright, perhaps from having saved a considerable amount of money, obtained a handsome bonus, made some good investments or received a substantial inheritance, most people purchase a home through the use of a home loan or mortgage on the property they wish to purchase.

Even those individuals who prefer not to borrow money will often rely on a mortgage when it comes to buying a place to live in, especially since the cost involved usually exceeds most people's available savings.

Furthermore, people contemplating purchasing their first house will typically need to get a mortgage loan that will be recorded and secured by a lien on their new home. These loans can be obtained from financial institutions like banks or sometimes from private sources like the seller of the property.

Home mortgages are usually characterized by an interest rate expressed as a annualized percentage rate or APR. The APR can be used by a mortgage shopper to compare different mortgages quotes of the same type at a quick glance.

Paying off a mortgage involves making regular payments each month that allow the house to be paid for over time. These payments can be fixed, as in fixed rate mortgages, or based upon some variable interest rate benchmark, as in adjustable rate mortgages.

The following sections will cover how to go about getting a mortgage to help pay for a home for you and/or your family to live in.

Getting a Mortgage

In order to get a mortgage, a prospective borrower will generally need to have accumulated a substantial lump sum of cash in savings to use as a down payment on the house they want to buy.

In addition, their credit rating will need to be sufficiently respectable to attract a financial institution that will lend them the balance required to make the home purchase.

Some people with an insufficient or negative credit history also choose to solicit a very creditworthy co-signer to guarantee their new mortgage loan. This is often a family member who trusts the borrower to make regular mortgage payments or who is willing to step in to make payments if the borrow gets in financial trouble for some reason in the future.

Types of Mortgage

When contemplating getting a mortgage, the first thing to realize is that most mortgages are either fixed rate or variable rate mortgages, although other types of mortgage, such as balloon mortgages may also be available to you.

If you would prefer the security of having to make a steady payment each month, then a fixed rate mortgage may be right for you. Getting a fixed rate mortgages can also be a good strategy when you think that mortgage interest rates are likely to rise over time.

Alternatively, if you prefer to pay a lower interest rate initially and are both willing and able to accept the risk of rising interest rates increasing your home payments, then a variable or adjustable rate mortgage may be suitable in your case. Obtaining a variable rate mortgage might also be an ideal strategy when you expect mortgage interest rates to fall over time.

Balloon mortgages might be used by someone that plans to sell their house and/or fully pay off their mortgage in the not too distant future, perhaps by refinancing at a lower rate once their credit rating improves. Such mortgages typically require relatively low monthly payments followed by a large lump sum to pay off the balance after a certain time frame.

Shopping for a Mortgage

Once you have decided to get a mortgage, you will need to go about finding the mortgage that is both right for your ability to pay and suitable for your prospective home. You may also need to boost your credit rating as much as possible in order to qualify for the most attractive mortgage rates.

Furthermore, since the annual percentage rates charged by mortgage lenders are generally different for fixed rate, variable rate and balloon mortgages, you will need to make sure that you do not try to compare the APR of one type of mortgage with the APR of another type of mortgage.

Then obtain a series of valid mortgage rate quotes from several different reputable mortgage lenders. Such quotes will generally be based on information about the property you are contemplating purchasing, your income and your proven ability and willingness to pay off loans as evidenced by your credit history.

Saving up for a Home Down Payment

If buying a new home at some point in the future seems to be the gold at the end of the rainbow for you, then you will probably want to start putting together a savings plan to accumulate enough money for a down payment.

For some people, putting together a home deposit worth tens of thousands of pounds may seem to be a daunting task, especially if they have never saved substantial amounts before.

Fortunately, saving up for a down payment on a new home does not have to be difficult, but it does take some time and advance planning in most cases. The following sections will discuss some of the steps you can take right away on your path toward amassing an appropriately sized down payment to make your dreams of a new home come true.

Doing Some Preliminary Research

In order to know roughly how much you will need to save up for a home down payment, you will want to take a look around the neighborhood you are most interested in purchasing a home in to see what desirable homes are for sale and what they typically cost.

You might also consider discussing your interest in saving for a home down payment with a local estate agent. They might be able to advise you about current real estate market conditions for the size and type of home you are most interested in purchasing.

The estate agent should also be familiar with prevailing price trends, just in case a substantial price rise or fall is anticipated that could substantially affect how much of a deposit you will need to accumulate.

Estimating the Amount You Need to Save

Now that you have done some research, use it to come up with an estimate of the likely price of a typical house you would like to own, and then have the price adjusted for the prevailing market trend.

The next step is to simply multiply the resulting expected house price by 20 percent to get the typical down payment required by most mortgage lenders before they will provide money toward a house purchase. This provides you with a target down payment amount you will need to save up.

Now that you have a target deposit amount, you will want to divide that amount by the number of years you are willing to wait in order to be able to afford your desired type of home. This will give you the amount of savings you will need to set aside each year for the home down payment.

Increase Earnings, Budget and Save Regularly

Once you know what about you need to save each year, you can set about putting the funds together in various ways. First of all, you can aim to maximize your income if you have any control over the amount of money you earn each month. Basically, the more money you earn, the more you can afford to save.

Next, you can assess your monthly needs and budget any spending appropriately so that more money is left over each month to be saved for your home down payment. You can also consider opening a special savings account for the planned home down payment so that you are less tempted to spend it.

Another important element of a long term savings plan is having the discipline to save money on a regular basis. You can do this by having a certain affordable amount deducted from your paycheck each month to be put toward your home down payment.

Finally, you will want to maximize the returns you earn on the money you set aside while saving for your home down payment. When investing your savings, remember to avoid sacrificing the security of knowing that your savings will eventually be returned to you safely so that they can be used for the intended purpose of buying a new home.

How to Save Money by Refinancing a Mortgage

The recent history of low interest rates have many home owners wondering if refinancing their home's mortgage loan might save them a considerable amount of money.

For example, if your mortgage was taken out five or more years ago, then computing what you could save by refinancing your mortgage could be a prudent way to save money on your future housing costs.

In general, a rate reduction of one percent or more on your home loan will tend to pay for the refinancing fees, closing costs and any points you might be paying up front. The following sections discuss additional aspects of how to save money by refinancing your mortgage.

When Refinancing Your Mortgage can Save You Money

In order to find out if refinancing your mortgage might save you money, first check mortgage rates online or call your bank to find out the current level of fixed or variable mortgage rates that you can use to compare with your current mortgage's interest rate. Make sure that you are comparing the same type of mortgage loan to the one you already have, such as fixed rate to fixed rate, or variable rate to variable rate.

You might want to think seriously about refinancing the mortgage loan on your home if mortgage rates have fallen considerably since you originally took out the loan, especially if comparable rates are more than one percent lower. Before refinancing, you will also want to make sure that you plan on staying in your current home for several years in order to make it an economic decision.

Also, remember to compute in advance roughly how much money you will save over time by paying a lower interest rate, compared to how much you will pay initially in refinancing fees to refinance your mortgage.

Shopping Around For a Refinancing Deal

Before shopping around for the best refinancing deal, you should first determine the type of new mortgage loan that you think would like to replace your old loan with. If you think interest rates are likely to rise substantially over the coming years, then you might prefer to look for a fixed rate loan. Alternatively, if you think mortgage rates are likely to stay the same or decline, then you might opt for a variable rate mortgage.

Once you know what kind of mortgage you want, checking the new relevant mortgage rate you will receive by refinancing your current home loan with several mortgage lenders can often really save you money. You can also contact a mortgage broker to provide you with advice and help you shop for the best and most suitable refinancing deal.

Another useful idea is calling up your existing mortgage holder or broker to ask whether they will help you refinance your current mortgage. Sometimes they will offer you a refinancing deal without the usual fees and costs that are commonly associated with the mortgage refinancing process, which can result in quite a substantial overall savings to you.

Paying Off Your Mortgage With Savings

Given the exceptionally low interest rates available on most legitimate savings accounts these days, many people have considered whether it would make sense to pay off some of the outstanding balance on their home mortgage, rather than hold their cash in a savings account or certificate of deposit.

Although mortgage rates have been making historic lows lately, the considerably lower rate of interest available on most savings accounts makes repaying a higher interest rate mortgage or home equity loan seem quite attractive.

Things to Consider Before Paying Off Your Mortgage With Savings

Of course, having a serious interest in pursuing a mortgage prepayment strategy using your savings would suggest that a person has first put sufficient money aside for emergencies and other long term goals in their savings account. The amount left over can then be used to pay down your mortgage.

Another important thing to take care of before using your savings to pay off your mortgage balance is paying off any higher interest rate debt that you have accumulated and still intend to repay. Unsecured debts might include credit card debt, as well as any private loans with interest rates higher than your mortgage rate. Higher interest rate secured debts such as car or motor home loans may also seem attractive to prepay before your mortgage.

Furthermore, some mortgages have a substantial pre-payment penalty that typically kicks in when you make a large lump sum payment before it is due. Call your mortgage lender and review your mortgage's terms and conditions to see if such a penalty might apply to the prepayment you have in mind, and whether you can fine tune your strategy to avoid paying a penalty unnecessarily.

Advantages of Using Savings to Pay off Your Mortgage

Perhaps the main advantage of paying off your mortgage balance earlier than required is to avoid having to make future interest rate payments that are higher than what you might receive on your savings account balances.

Computing the difference between your mortgage interest rate and your after-tax savings interest rate will help you get a good sense for how much money you will probably save each year by paying off your mortgage balance early.

Prepaying your mortgage balance will also typically mean that you can own your home outright and become mortgage free within a shorter period of time. Eliminating the mortgage cost burden as quickly as possible often makes it considerably easier for people to retire early.

Options for Paying Off Your Mortgage Balance

Once you have paid off higher interest rate debts and have decided that your excess savings are best used to pay off your mortgage, the next logical step would be to approach your mortgage holder to discuss your prepayment options.

For example, you might be able to pay off a lump sum from your overall outstanding mortgage balance by emptying out a savings account or cashing in a certificate of deposit that you no longer find necessary to hold.

Alternatively, you could instead make regular additional prepayments each month along with your usually mortgage payment that will be steadily deducted from your balance. This might suit a saver that does not have a lump sum, but who can instead allocate additional funds from each paycheck to prepay their mortgage.

CHAPTER 9: PERSONAL LOAN AND CREDIT CARD TIPS

For this chapter, the reader is again reminded about these very wise words attributed to Shakespeare: "Neither a borrower nor a lender be because loan oft loses both itself and friend, and borrowing dulls the edge of husbandry."

Personal loans are often a touchy subject for people who have been burned by lack of repayment of a loan they extended to someone they trusted. If you lend money to a friend in need, will they still be considered your friend if they fail to repay the loan? Those unable to repay personal loans will often avoid meeting or speaking to the person they borrowed from out of embarrassment and a desire to avoid confronting their lender.

Furthermore, as Benjamin Franklin once reportedly put it, "Creditors have better memories than debtors." This fact of life argues strongly for putting any personal loan agreement in writing to have a legally-binding form of documented evidence.

This important loan formality can help eliminate any memory-related issues over what was owed to whom and under precisely what terms it was lent before an expensive lawsuit or other legal action results from the lender's failed attempts at debt collection.

It generally therefore seems far better to avoid making loans to others unless you first fully prepared yourself to lose both the money and perhaps even the friendship and companionship of the borrower. Similarly, those taking out such loans may also lose a friend if they become unable to repay the person they borrowed from.

On the other hand, making or taking out personal loans secured by an asset that the lender would willingly accept in case of a default might make some sense since the lender will at least have something desirable to compensate themselves with if the loaned money does not come back to them for some reason. Such an agreement should also be put in writing.

Furthermore, a large number of people have gotten themselves buried under a heavy load of credit card debt that they paid high interest rates on and eventually became unable to repay at all.

If you fail to make a payment on a credit card loan, and the interest rate then rises to over 20 percent, as is the case with many credit card loans, just think about whether you will ever be able to repay that loan fully in order to avoid long-term damage to your credit rating.

Rather than fall prey to the temptation of the easy money that a credit card can provide, it seems far preferable to resolve to live entirely within your means as provided by your existing income. That usually involves focusing on spending money on what you actually need and expanding your income as necessary.

You will also want to plan on saving up extra money by using the money-saving advice contained in this book for major purchases of things you want to add to your life or your family's lives or for anticipated future expenditures.

For very important reasons like those detailed above, anyone contemplating making or requesting an unsecured personal loan or becoming indebted to credit card companies are strongly advised to think again and to avoid the temptation to borrow if at all possible.

These crucial personal finance topics and the excellent reasons behind

GREAT MONEY SAVING TIPS

this sound advice will be covered in greater depth in the following sections.

Tips on Making a Personal Loan

As discussed above, making personal loans can be a risky way to invest your money if you do not follow some basic guidelines designed to keep your money as safe as possible.

Furthermore, whenever lending money to friends, business associates or family members, remember that you also take the risk of losing their friendship if the money is not repaid promptly.

The following sections include four top tips often recommended by financial advisors and lawyers that you would be well advised to take into account whenever making personal loans.

Get the Personal Loan Agreement in Writing

Some people may keep to an oral agreement to repay money, but when you need to enforce a loan agreement, it is always best to have it written down in the form of a signed promissory note so that it can be used to prove that a loan was indeed made.

In such written agreements, you will typically state the names of the borrower and lender, where and when the loan was made, the amount of the loan, any interest charges that may result from the loan, and the loan's repayment terms.

The personal loan agreement might also include what the loan will be used for, as well as a description of any security that is being pledged by the borrower to the lender in case the loan cannot be repaid as originally planned. Also remember to keep a copy of any check used to make the personal loan.

Secure Any Personal Loan Well

You typically have a much better chance of your money coming back to you from a personal loan if you secure the loan by taking possession of or a lien against an item of considerable value relative to the size of the loan.

For example, you can lend money in a personal loan secured against a piece of real estate or a car. Another idea is to allow the borrower to secure their personal loan on some especially valuable jewelry that you can hold in your possession until the loan is repaid.

A good rule of thumb is to secure the loan by having the borrower give or pledge to you an item or piece of property that is reasonably worth at least twice the amount of money that you will be lending in the personal loan.

Get a Second Opinion

Obtaining competent advice about any loan you are contemplating could save you considerable worry and stress in the long run, not to mention money.

Many people prefer to have any substantial written personal loan agreement looked over by a lawyer before signing it. This legal review helps assure that the agreement will be legally binding on the borrower in order to secure your financial interests and that you are not agreeing to anything inadvisable.

Do Your Homework

To avoid falling prey to loan fraud and other scams, make sure you do some research about the borrower, their credentials and their creditworthiness before lending them any money in a personal loan.

At a minimum, you really need to know who they are, where they live, and how to contact them by telephone and mail. You can usually do this by asking them for these details, and by obtaining a color copy of the borrower's photo identification.

Another excellent idea is to obtain the potential borrower's financial details and run a detailed copy of their credit report. By doing this, you can see if any adverse credit reports have been made that should give you pause before lending them any significant sum of money.

Five Great Tips for Using Credit Cards

Those who are relatively new to using credit cards could typically benefit from being aware of some useful basic tips for using credit cards appropriately and dealing with the companies that issue their credit cards.

Such guidelines can help you avoid common pitfalls that can damage your credit rating and can also result in excessive and expensive unsecured debt balances accumulated by using your credit card unwisely.

Remembering the following five tips can really help you save money and keep out of trouble when using credit cards:

Tip#1: Pay on Time

Credit card interest rates typically go through the roof when you either miss a payment or are late when making one.

Even if you only pay the minimum amount required, be sure that you make the payment on time. This can also help you avoid having to pay late fees.

Tip#2: Read Your Agreement

Some people neglect to read the fine print in their credit card agreement before signing it. This can result in costly charges when they unwittingly break the rules that their credit card company expects them to abide by.

Avoid having this happen to you by reading your credit card agreement thoroughly. Make a summary of the key points in the agreement that you will need to keep to in order to avoid paying extra or having your credit rating damaged by an unfavorable report.

Tip#3: Negotiate

If you have been an excellent credit card customer with an impeccable payment record established over a considerable period of time, do not hesitate to negotiate with your credit card company to reduce your interest rate.

You may also be eligible for some other credit card perks reserved for favored customers, so call them up and ask what you might qualify for.

Also, if you have to miss a payment for some good reason and your interest rate shoots up as a result, you can sometimes negotiate a reduction in this rate by contacting your credit card company.

Tip#4: Transfer Balances

Some credit cards offer especially low APRs for a limited time frame as a special incentive to attract new customers.

If you are routinely running a credit card balance, consider transferring the outstanding balance to a new lower interest rate credit card account when your lower interest rate time period expires.

Make sure that you compute how much you will be saving by such a transfer after taking into account any extra fees or costs involved.

Tip#5: Forgo Cash Advances

Taking out cash advances from your credit card account are often considerably more expensive than just using your credit card to make a purchase, if possible.

Also, unless you really need to take a cash advance from your credit card account for an emergency, try to keep a sufficient balance in your checking account instead.

This way, you can just use a quick ATM debit card withdrawal or cash a check to cover an unanticipated need for cash that you may have been tempted to use a credit card cash advance for.

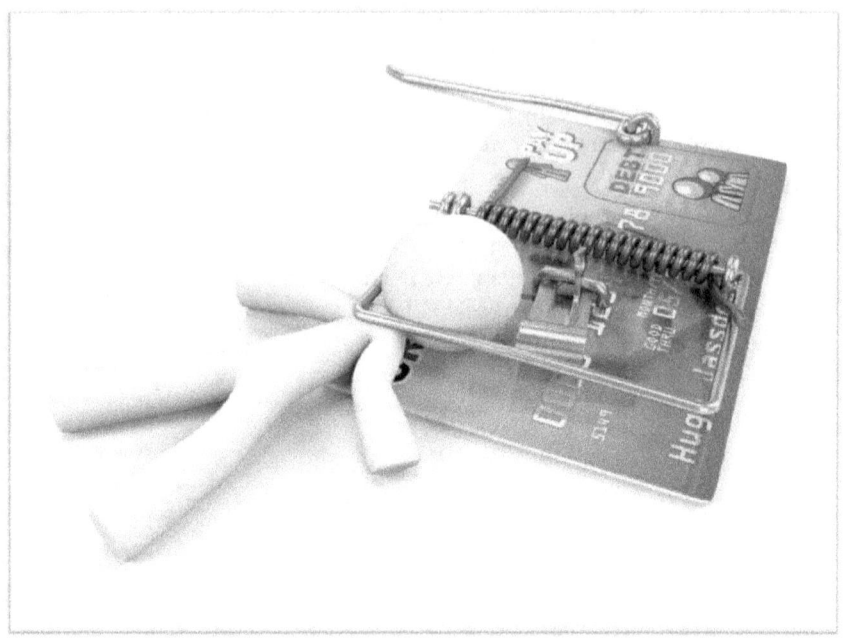

Avoiding the Traps of Credit Card Pitfalls

Since the imprudent use of credit cards can quickly destroy the credit rating of the unwary spender, anyone who uses credit cards should learn how to avoid the most common credit card pitfalls.

Furthermore, although credit card companies and banks that issue credit cards typically do not want you to know this, the financial risks involved in using credit cards to make purchases can be considerable.

The following sections discuss some of the primary credit card pitfalls so that you can plan on avoiding these financially-hazardous traps.

Why Credit Card Pitfalls Cause Problems

Most credit card pitfalls occur when people have a tendency to exceed the limits of their ability to repay the debt incurred by their use of credit cards. For example, they might either use credit cards to pay for emergency expenses or to purchase luxuries that they cannot really afford.

Of course, the actual use of the credit card itself — which are readily accepted by almost all major retailers and service companies — is relative quick, easy and painless. Nevertheless, most of the problems associated with using credit cards tend to arise with the credit card bill.

Avoid Running Credit Card Balances

Basically, if the credit card's balance is not paid off promptly each and every month, then substantial credit card balances can accrue surprisingly quickly. It can take many years to pay off even a modest credit card balance by paying just the account's minimum payment each month.

If the consumer then keeps on spending beyond their means, this situation often puts unwary credit card holders in serious danger of getting into a burdensome debt situation that they simply cannot afford to get out of without a default, especially if they are ever late on a credit card payment.

Avoid Making Late Payments on Credit Card Accounts

Late payments are typically used as an opportunity for credit card issuers to penalize the borrower by boosting the interest rate the cardholder has to pay on balances.

Depending on the applicable credit card agreement, a borrower being late on a credit card payment can trigger their credit card issuer to raise the interest rate charged on unpaid credit card balances from the rather affordable and attractive five to ten percent range into the increasingly unaffordable 20-30 percent region.

Once that dramatic rate hike has happened, some credit card borrowers gradually slip into a default situation where they stop making payments altogether on their credit card balances. This is the point at which the borrower's credit rating starts to suffer dramatically due to the resulting adverse credit reports made to the major credit agencies.

Avoid Exchanging Unsecured Debt for Secured Debt

If a large credit card balance has accrued or a default has already occurred, some people are tempted or even advised by debt reduction specialists to exchange their high interest rate unsecured credit card balances for a lower interest rate loan secured against one of their major assets, such as their house, motor home or car.

Although this exchange can make it easier and faster for the debt-burdened borrower to repay the credit card debt, it presents yet another pitfall for the unwary credit card consumer. Since the nature of an unsecured debt is that it is only backed by the creditworthiness of the borrower, this means that damage to their credit rating is the primary risk of default.

Nevertheless, securing a debt with a valuable physical asset typically allows the lender to foreclose on, take possession of, and/or put a lien on a physical asset that may allow the lender to force a sale of the asset, usually at a very disadvantageous price.

As a result, securing your previously unsecured credit card debt with your home or primary means of transport can leave you without these very useful assets if you remain unable to pay off the debt as promised.

CHAPTER 10: RETIREMENT SAVINGS TIPS

Government pension plans in developed countries have become increasingly stressed by an aging population that is both living longer and having fewer children. Many people also choose to supplement their public pension by purchasing an annuity to provide them with a steady retirement income for their remaining lifetime.

Putting some money aside as savings for retirement either to live on or to purchase a suitable annuity with makes more sense than ever in this challenging financial environment. This seems especially true since public pension cuts look increasingly likely in future.

Basically, elderly people will probably have to rely even more on their savings to support their chosen retirement lifestyle, so the time to start preparing for your retirement is now. If you have not yet started a retirement savings plan, you can make doing so one of your new savings resolutions.

The following sections of this chapter contain some helpful tips about saving money for retirement.

Compute How Much You Will Need

A number of variables will affect how much you will need to have saved by your retirement to maintain your chosen lifestyle for the remainder of your expected lifetime.

These factors include the anticipated rate of inflation, the expected level of low risk interest rates, projected annuity costs, your intended retirement age, and the payment level of any public or private pension plans you may qualify for.

Furthermore, if you own your home, you may also be able to sell it and rent or gradually draw down on your investment in that asset over time to supplement your retirement income. This should be included in your retirement needs calculation.

You can use a spreadsheet like Microsoft's Excel, an online pension calculator, or the services of a professional retirement advisor to compute how much you are likely to need to have set aside by your chosen retirement age in order to achieve the post-retirement income stream you want.

Once you know how much money you need to save for retirement and by what age you will need to have saved it, figure out how much money you will need to set aside each month in order to achieve that goal. A simple calculation involves dividing the amount you intend to save by the number of months remaining until your retirement.

Set Money Aside Regularly and When Lump Sums Arrive

After you have determined how much you need to save each month, open up a special retirement account to hold your retirement savings in.

Next, arrange to have that needed amount of money taken out of your paycheck each and every month to be deposited directly into your retirement savings account.

Avoid having a debit card linked to your retirement savings account, since you do not want to be making withdrawals, just deposits.

You may even qualify for a tax deferred retirement savings account to which you can contribute up to a certain amount each year. Your tax accountant can advise you further on benefitting from such accounts.

If you obtain a lump sum of cash from an employment bonus, asset sale or inheritance, then some portion of such larger amounts can also be stashed away into your retirement savings account.

Invest Your Retirement Savings Wisely

Once you have begun to save for retirement, be sure to put most of the money you accumulate into stable and secure financial investments to help keep your nest egg safe. For most people, this means having a retirement savings account or certificates of deposit placed only with very creditworthy financial institutions.

Of course, to beat the persistent rate of inflation, you might also want to place some of your retirement portfolio's funds into higher yielding growth assets. The price of such investments can go up or down, so you need to be willing to assume the risk involved.

This portion of your retirement portfolio might allocate capital to include the purchase of riskier investments like stocks, high yield corporate bonds and precious metals.

To avoid the challenge involved in picking assets to invest in over the long term, some people planning for their retirement prefer to put some of their money into one or more mutual funds to allow professional fund managers to choose their investments instead.

CHAPTER 11: PARTING ADVICE

Basically, when it comes to saving money, knowledge really is power. By knowing how save money in the first place by educating yourself thoroughly on the topic, you can save more money and generate the financial power you need to get what you most want out of life.

This goal can be achieved by doing constructive things like reading this book for a general introduction to the topic and speaking to knowledgeable people for their financial advice. You can also research money saving tips on the Internet regarding areas of your life where you think you can cut costs.

Furthermore, you then need to perform the critical step of applying that money saving knowledge you have gained from your research in as consistent a manner as possible in your daily life. If you make mistakes when it comes to saving money, as just about everyone does, do your best to refrain from being too harsh on yourself. Just resolve instead to do better in future and to learn from your errors.

To refresh your memory about the pitfalls you fell into and avoided on your path to financial freedom, it may help you to keep a journal about saving money that you can refer back to from time to time for helpful tips and to remember what mistakes you made and kept yourself from making.

You will also have to remember to practice restraint in your spending habits in order to control and suppress your impulses to satisfy your desires instead of focusing on fulfilling your needs. This remains one of the key elements to saving money successfully that should be your new focus, so always ask yourself if you really need something before spending any money on it.

Finally, having the discipline to do the things that save you money will generally distinguish successful savers from the rest of the pack. The outcome of this money saving process will typically get you much closer to achieving your financial goals faster as you start the process of providing a secure monetary foundation and sense of financial freedom for your own life and that of any others who depend on you for support.

ABOUT THE AUTHORS

Jay and Julie Hawk are a husband and wife writing team who currently also manage money as part of The FXperts team of financial experts. Together, they have more than 40 years of professional experience in the financial arena, and they have both spent over a decade writing on financial topics.

After both independently retiring from their professional financial careers as relatively wealthy people, Jay and Julie met up, fell love and got married to raise a child together just after the new millennium dawned. They moved to Mexico to semi-retire near the beach and operate an Internet-based business together.

Their experience there involved living in a neighborhood of people who were typically less well-off than they were. This gave them considerable insight into what things were truly necessary in life, the importance of saving money, and how to cut costs and still enjoy a wonderful life living and working together.

They also often found their deep financial knowledge very helpful to manage their own money with, to advise their family with about investments, and to help out friends who had retired to the same region and needed sound financial advice to manage their retirement funds with.

Since they were looking for a way to work remotely due to the rather weak local economy, they eventually started a new career together as freelance writers specializing in writing about the financial markets and other financial topics using their professional background and expertise.

This resulted in them co-founding The FXperts to provide clients with expertly-written financial market analysis, commentary and informational content as well as trader mentoring, account management and financial consulting services.

As a result of their life experiences and accumulated financial wisdom, they felt it would be beneficial to share their substantial knowledge with a broader audience. Jay and Julie are now very pleased to present this book on saving money as a practical compliment to their other financial books published by Jellyhawk Financial Press. These include a two-part series of books on technical and fundamental financial market analysis, as well as a three volume guide to trading the forex, stock and commodity markets.

You can visit The FXperts' website at www.thefxperts.com to find links to purchase their other books and learn about their future book releases.

INDEX

Account balance, 26
Acetic acid, 61
Acquisition impulse, 47
Advertising, 44
Advertising, 43, 44
Advice, 127
Alcohol, 55
Aloe Vera, 56
Assets, 19
Authors, 129
Auto repairs, 65
Baking soda, 60, 61
Bank, 25, 29
Benjamin Franklin, 111
Bills, 38
Budget, 20, 47, 104
Cancer, 56
Car, 39
Cash Advances, 118
Cell Phones, 68
Charity, 59
Chemical residues, 60
Child Care, 77, 78
Child Minders, 78
Cleaning, 61
Cleaning Products, 60, 63

Clothing, 57
Coconut oil, 61
Consignment shop, 59
Consumer goods, 47
Cooking, 50
Cornstarch, 61
Cost-cutting, 2, 35
Coupons, 53
Credentials, 41
Credit card, 111, 117, 120
Cutting costs, 37
Debt, 17, 20, 23
Deodorant, 61
Deposit accounts, 29
Diet, 55
Dining out, 52
Discipline, 36, 58
Discounts, 53
Dividend, 31
Down Payment, 103
Drinks, 52
Drugs, 54, 55
Eating less, 50
Education, 17, 58
Electricity, 38
Electronics, 72

Emergencies, 4
Emergency, 16, 25
Energy, 71
Entertainment, 57, 81
Equities, 31
Equity funds, 31
Essential oils, 61
Exercising, 55
Expenses, 23, 39
Family, 60, 75
Fasting, 50
FDIC. *See* Federal Deposit Insurance Corporation
Fed Funds Rate, 28
Federal Deposit Insurance Corporation, 30
Federal Reserve, 2
Financial Confidence, 5
Financial Plan, 13, 14, 32
Financial planner, 14
Financial planning, 14
Financial predators, 40
Financial profiling, 13
Financial Services Compensation Scheme, 29
Flea markets, 58
Food, 38, 83
Freedom, 46
Frugality, 4
FSCS. *See* Financial Services Compensation Scheme
Funeral, 92, 93
Garage sale, 59
Gift spending, 87
Gilts, 30
Goals, 20
Good Samaritan, 5
Google Voice, 70
Grandparents, 89
Greasy stains, 61
Great Recession, 28
Great tips, 32, 36
Greed, 41

Health, 54, 60
Health conditions, 55
Healthy, 55
Healthy eating, 55
Healthy weight, 55
Heating, 71
Holiday, 87
Holiday Meals, 83
Holiday Spending, 86
Home Remedies, 55
Hotels, 81
House, 38
Housing, 38
Hydrogen peroxide, 56, 60, 62
Impulse, 58
Impulse purchases, 46
Individual Savings Accounts, 29
Inheritance, 37, 95, 96
Interest rates, 29
Internet, 27, 44, 55
Internet telephony, 69
Investing, 7, 8
Investments, 42
ISA. *See* Individual Savings Accounts
Jay and Julie Hawk, xii
Jay Hawk, 129
Jellyhawk Financial Press, ii, ix, 130
Julie Hawk, 129
Late payments, 121
Laundry detergent, 62
Leftovers, 85
LIBOR. *See* London Inter-Bank Offered Rate
Lifestyle, 38
Loan agreement, 114
London Inter-Bank Offered Rate, 26
Luxuries, 37, 38
Meals, 49
Mechanics, 66
Medicaid, 54

Medical expenses, 54
Medicare, 54
Meditation, 55
Money saving, 49, 57
Money saving plan, 35
Money saving tips, 35
Moody's, 30
Mortgage, 101, 106, 108
Multivitamin, 55
Mutual funds, 31
National Health Service, 54
Nest egg, 31
Netflix, 45
Official Bank Rate, 28
Official registration, 41
Oxfam, 58
Personal loan, 111, 114, 115
Personal spending coach, xi
Pesticides, 55
Pets, 60
Plant-based diet, 51, 56
Potluck, 84
Processed foods, 50
Protein, 51
Refinancing, 106, 107
Refrigerators, 72
Repair, 47
Resolutions, 22
Restaurant, 52, 81
Retirement, 17, 123, 125
Return, 28, 41
Rubbing alcohol, 60
Salt, 60
Salvation Army, 58
Save money, 43, 52, 61
Saving, 2, 7
Saving goals, 19

Saving money, 1, 8, 10, 16, 32, 40, 46, 54, 57, 60
Saving priorities, 16
Saving rate, 22
Savings account, 3, 25, 26, 29, 35
Savings objectives, 47
Savings plan, 44
Savings program, 37
Scammer, 41
Scams, 40, 41
Second hand, 57
Second hand goods, 47
Secured debt, 121
Shopping tips, 46
Skype, 70
Sodium bicarbonate, 61
Spending less, 37
Spending money, 23
Standard and Poor's, 30
Stocks, 31
Tax, 96
Tax deduction, 59
Taxes, 20
Telephone, 38
Television, 44
The FXperts, 130
Tips, 57
Tobacco, 55
Toothpaste, 60
U.S. Treasury Bonds, 30
Unsecured Debt, 121
Vacations, 38, 80
White vinegar, 61
Work, 54
Yard sales, 58
Yield curve, 30
YouTube, 45

www.ingramcontent.com/pod-product-compliance
Lightning Source LLC
Chambersburg PA
CBHW052301220526
45471CB00001B/437